PENGUIN BOOKS
PRIVATE LIVES

Bettina Arndt was brought up and educated in Canberra, and gained a BSc from the Australian National University. She was later awarded a Master of Psychology degree for her research into the treatment of female orgasmic dysfunction.

Bettina Arndt has worked as a clinical psychologist, specialising in sexual therapy. She was a consultant to (and later publisher of) *Forum* magazine, and is now involved with postgraduate medical courses, training seminars, and giving lectures to self-help groups and community organisations.

She writes for a range of magazines: *Cleo*, *Mode*, the *Bulletin*, *Playboy* and *Australian Women's Weekly*; and also appears regularly on radio and television.

Private Lives

Bettina Arndt

To Tim & Martha,

with thanks
for all your
valuable contacts,

Bettina Arndt

Penguin Books Australia Ltd,
487 Maroondah Highway, P.O. Box 257
Ringwood, Victoria 3134, Australia
Penguin Books Ltd,
Harmondsworth, Middlesex, England
Penguin Books,
40 West 23rd Street, New York, N.Y. 10010, U.S.A.
Penguin Books (Canada) Limited,
2801 John Street, Markham, Ontario, Canada L3R 1B4
Penguin Books (N.Z.) Ltd,
182-190 Wairau Road, Auckland 10, New Zealand

First published by Penguin Books Australia, 1986
Reprinted 1986

Copyright © Bettina Arndt, 1986
Bettina Arndt is managed by Harry M. Miller and Company Management

Typeset in Paladium by Midland Typesetters Pty Ltd, Maryborough
Made and printed in Australia by
The Dominion Press-Hedges & Bell, Maryborough

CIP

Arndt, Bettina.
Private lives.

ISBN 0 14 008850 4.

1. Life skills. 2. Sex instruction. 3. Mental health.
I. Title.

158'.1

Dedicated with love and gratitude to my friend Judy Black, who has heightened the highs and softened the lows in my life. I thank her for her endless patience, wisdom, support and concern.

Acknowledgements

Many of these articles have been previously published, but have been revised for this book. The dates and places of publication (in the order the pieces appear in this book) are listed as follows:

'Loved Husband' (*Sydney Morning Herald* and the *Age*, 24 October 1981; 'Bare Body Comfort' (*Cleo*, June 1984); 'Sex, Pregnancy and Motherhood' (*Cleo*, November 1984); 'Men and Marriage' (*Bulletin*, 16 April 1985); 'The Devastation of Divorce' (*Bulletin*, 25 June 1985); 'The Man Shortage' (*Bulletin*, 21 May 1985); 'Single Women' (*Cleo*, July 1983); 'The Mateship Myth' (*Bulletin*, 21 January 1986); 'Confessions of a Superwoman' (*Mode*, May 1984); 'The Contented Workaholic' (*Bulletin*, 8 October 1985); 'Masculinity is a Health Hazard' (*Cleo*, January 1984); 'Executive Sex' (*Australian Business Review*, 2 September 1982); 'Impotence' (*Bulletin*, 25 October 1983); 'A Revolution in Sex' (*Cleo*, November 1982); 'Sexual Worlds Apart' (*Cleo*, December 1984); 'Giving Sex a Bad Name . . .' (*Cleo*, March 1983); 'Blat Sex' (*Cleo*, July 1984); 'Man and His Penis' (*Cleo*, July 1984); 'Sexual Ages of Women' (*Cleo*, April 1983); 'Lone Fathers' (*Australian Women's Weekly*, March 1983); and 'Gay Children' (*Australian Women's Weekly*, October 1984).

Contents

Introduction

I always did have a problem with distance. Professional distance, that is. The detachment a proper psychologist is supposed to maintain between her clients and herself. An ability to rationally and impersonally dissect other people's lives; to stand back, observe, modify behaviour without becoming personally involved.

Actually, that's what led me into sex in the first place. There I was, training to be a clinical psychologist, trying to acquire professional detachment when all of a sudden I found my personal life, my personal experiences pushing me in quite a different direction. It was in a seminar with a small group of other psychologists, mainly males. We were discussing female masturbation, namely why it was that relatively few young women (less than a third at the time) discover masturbation and learn to reach orgasm through self-stimulation. The males dominated the discussion; 'they have this aversion to touching themselves', 'they are anxious about this', 'they fear that'.

I sat there listening until I could no longer control myself, and then blurted out, 'I can never remember masturbating while I was a teenager. It never occurred to me to do it but I don't think I had any deep-seated fears or anxieties . . .' All the male eyebrows were raised, suspicions aroused, and they spent the next two hours cross-examining me, trying to find my deep-seated aversion to my genitals. My personal experience was dismissed as irrelevant, my arguments were unscientific, too emotional, too personal.

It infuriated me, and inspired me to conduct research into female masturbation, explaining the reasons why so many women like myself had simply never stumbled across a sexual activity which was so familiar to most males. In the process I listened to ninety women talking about the intimate details of their sexual lives and found it increasingly difficult to simply play the voyeur. Rather than forcing them to expose themselves in front of a stranger, it was natural to occasionally move away from the professional role of observer, to get out from behind the desk and let them know that I shared many of the anxieties, had some of the same experiences.

With sexual problems, there was little risk in revealing I'd been in the same boat – feeling similarly embarrassed, ignorant or confused. Many sex therapists do this – there's no harm in admitting that you, too, masturbate and feel guilty about it, that orgasms aren't always easy, erections can be elusive. It's part of breaking down the myth that sex experts are people who do it all perfectly. They don't, they just have a few answers as to how to get back on the right track when you have wandered off. They know – because they've usually been there themselves.

So by the time I moved from being a sex therapist to talking publicly about sex, working on radio, television, to publishing *Forum* magazine, it was natural to expose myself. Having chosen not to play the detached expert dealing face-to-face with people's problems, there seemed little point in becoming more removed, simply because I was now talking to not one, but thousands of people. On radio I'd find myself exchanging personal stories, ideas or thoughts about sex with my listeners, the intimacy of a talk-back programme creating such an illusion of privacy that you'd forget the world was listening. My friends listening would tell me later that they could pick the moment I'd suddenly realise I was talking publicly about something I'd later regret – they'd hear me hesitate and then plunge on, knowing it was far too late to get cold feet.

With experience and continued exposure, eventually almost all my personal barriers surrounding sex came down. What for most people is the most intimate, private part of their lives, for me became one of the most comfortable and most public.

The next step came accidentally. My decision to publicly expose other intimate aspects of my life was far from deliberate. In the midst of coping with the sudden death of my husband in late 1981, I was surprised to find myself obsessed by a desire to write down all the confused thoughts I had about his death and the effects on our family. It started off as a letter to a friend, and ended up as an article published in newspapers, specifically the *Age*. It was partly vengeance, anger at the *Age* for the meagre obituary they'd given my husband Dennis, who'd worked for the newspaper for many years and had ended up as one of their feature writers.

I had never really written while Dennis was alive. I was intimidated by his skilful writing and persuaded him to ghost for me the few published articles that appeared before then, including the editorials for our magazine, *Forum*. So 'Loved Husband' was the beginning – written out of anger, and with little thought of the risks. It led to a new career – writing for magazines in the Consolidated Press group – the *Bulletin*, *Cleo*, *Women's Weekly*, *Mode*. When I was forced to close *Forum* magazine mid-1982, 'Loved Husband' was my entrée into the world of journalism.

So personal tragedy became the inspiration for an article which would never have been written at a calmer, less vulnerable time. But then, having exposed such raw wounds so publicly, there seemed little point in holding back. I spend now much of my time writing and talking about general social issues, relationships – and, of course, sex. Yet occasionally, when an issue hits a raw nerve in my own personal life, there seems little point in pretending to be dispassionate and uninvolved. Some of these articles were obviously written at a specific time of my life, some have been revised for this book – but I hope that one way or another most touch on my own experiences.

Having made the decision to write about things so close to home, it is amazing how my own personal life has managed to embrace so many of the current issues affecting our society. A friend of mine once was reading Gail Sheehy's book *Passages* which describes major life events and how they influence adult development. She commented on the fact that I had done it all – raced through all the major passages just over the first decade of my adult life. It was true – single, then married with two step children, my own child, widowed, then single again – this time as a lone parent, and finally remarriage.

Whatever else it has done for me, there's plenty of inspiration there for writing about social issues. But occasionally you wonder what you do to your life by living it once and then rehashing it publicly for all to pick over. In moulding private events for public consumption, people you have known and loved are publicly lumbered with your version of what took place. Having learnt this, sometimes painfully, I now take more care to protect what's left of my private life . . . and theirs.

Close to Home

How It Began

*I*t was just after the first piece in this section, 'Loved Husband', was published in the newspapers I received a phone call from a woman in Queensland. 'I've just read your article,' she said, 'I had to ring you and tell you. I've always hated you.'

You get used to this type of reaction when you talk publicly about sex. It turned out that I had once lectured her daughter, a medical student, on common sexual practices and the mother was horrified to learn that I'd mentioned oral sex. But what was surprising about this particular phone call was the woman was so amazed to learn from my article that I was a mother, a step-mother and a recent widow that she felt inspired to ring and tell me she'd changed her mind about me. In one fell swoop, I'd moved from black to white. It was so disconcerting to find out that you can be blackballed simply by mentioning a common sexual practice – and then be forgiven when it is discovered you are just like other people, and share the same problems.

The article, focussing mainly on the difficulties of establishing a new family involving stepchildren, obviously touched a raw nerve for many people in a similar situation. Judging from the response I received, there was obviously much comfort to be gained from the fact that I, as a psychologist, also found it all heavy going.

The better known I become, the more it seems to make sense to write personally and show other people I share many of their conflicts and confusions, and take pleasure in many of the things they do. There are particular areas, like the experience of being a mother, that all too often are ignored by female journalists keen to make it into the big time by avoiding the 'soft' issues which so often are relegated to the women's pages. I've been lucky, with my professional background, to have been able to work it the other way. To force a soft issue . . . like men and marriage, or male friendships, into a hard news magazine (even if it means dressing up the research with facts and figures to make it more palatable for stitched-up male readers).

But in the end, it's writing about our 'private' lives that I really prefer. It's so rewarding to have the chance to write and talk publicly about many of the issues that privately concern me and my friends . . . and then to receive feedback from women (and men) all over Australia about their reactions. It is a treat to run into young mothers in supermarkets who tell me they were reassured to find they weren't the only ones to lose interest in sex following the birth of their child. They are delighted to discover that I, too, have cellulite on my thighs, and once stuffed my father's socks into my empty bra.

It's nice to know that publicly revealing my personal warts does appear to give solace to others sharing the same afflictions. One thing's certain – it makes people feel that they can tell me anything and everything . . . and they do. Most of the time, it's rather nice, even if it sometimes means that you step into a taxi and are immediately told the intimate details of the driver's sex life, or end up counselling the furniture removalist in between shifting piles of belongings from house to house.

There *are* times when it causes problems, when the public life intrudes a little too far into the personal. There I was, with all the other mums, supervising our children at a swimming lesson. Up popped this man who, without a word of introduction, proceeded to ask me if I thought his wife had left him because of the snakes on his bottom. He had these tattoos, you see, snake tattoos stretching from his shoulders right down to wrap lovingly around his buttocks. Oh dear, swimming lessons will never be quite the same after that . . .

Loved Husband

Last month [October 1981] an obituary appeared in the Melbourne newspaper, the *Age*. An obituary? Well, six sentences, a couple of paragraphs which a lot of people may have missed. After all, they only made the second edition of the newspaper.

'Dennis Minogue, former feature writer . . . worked for the *Age* in the early 1960s and from 1973-1976' – a few facts squeezed as an afterthought into the 'In Brief' section in the newspaper.

The last paragraph . . . 'Mr Minogue is survived by his wife and three children.' They got it wrong. The only thing which really mattered, they got wrong.

Two days before, I stood in our kitchen while friends tried to help to compose a notice for the obituary columns of the newspapers, the *Sydney Morning Herald* and the *Age*. 'Loved husband of Bettina, father of Jesse, Kate and Daniel,' they suggested. They laughed, embarrassed at my suggestion we change it to 'loved husband of Bettina and Johanna, father of etc,' but finally accepted with relief the more acceptable compromise, the editor's touch – 'dearly loved by Bettina, Johanna, Kate, Daniel and Jesse.'

When the details of the full financial catastrophe started to unfold, the burden which, in dark nights I feel led to Dennis's heart attack, descends upon me. How could I support two homes, Johanna, Dennis's first wife and two children, my son Jesse now six months – two mortgages, two sets of car insurance, two sets of medical benefits, two of everything . . . 'She's not your responsibility,' 'Isn't she working now?' ' She'll just have to pull her weight,' they all say.

My days now are parcelled, cut into five-minute intervals. Feeding Jesse, he plays for a minute – time to get dressed? Best not, wail till he's asleep after breakfast. A desperate scurry around the house then ready to meet an onslaught of decisions – about print runs, layouts, meetings with bank managers, a hunt through years of files looking for answers which Dennis took with him. And in all this a gnawing need to leave some time for the children – Dennis's children who, after seven years of anger and resentment, I learnt to love.

Kate and Daniel know this as their home. 'Take this (toy, book) home with you,' someone said when they were here last week. 'This is my home,' said Kate fiercely.

Kate yesterday babbled on to me about rearranging the bedrooms when Jesse is older so that the two boys can live together in the attic when Jesse is four or five, Daniel then twelve or thirteen.

This is her world, Jesse is her brother, I am her – stepmother? Her friend? Her father's love?

Last week she asked me what I was going to do with her father's clothes. We talked and I tried to find out if she wanted anything that was his for herself. Her reply was hesitant and then it came out. If I died, would I leave her – what to her were the obvious symbols of our love – my wedding ring and the pendant Dennis chose for me to wear on the day of our wedding.

The strange thing is that Kate was the hardest. Kate, who at age ten now mothers me and tells me she loves me. Kate, whom I trust to lift my precious, heavy, squirming son from his cot. Kate was our real test. Kate was almost two when Dennis left. She was the child Dennis and Johanna longed for after the first baby died at birth. She was for many years the saviour of that marriage, the most important reason Dennis came home between his endless travelling, his relentless wandering as foreign correspondent. Kate remembers the years in which her father lived out of a suitcase – a few months with her, her mother, Daniel the baby and then months when he was away, living with me.

Living with me – exhilarating, joyful days when we discovered each other, shared our dreams, talked of the future and then the nights when I would awake to hear Dennis sobbing in his sleep calling out Kate's name.

Kate remembers the first meetings with me, the stranger whom she knew her mother hated. She clung to her father, pushed herself between us when we touched. She remembers the picnics, the trips to the zoo, the first days after Johanna gave in and allowed Dennis to have the children for a few hours and then a day. Dennis's desperate attempts to play happy families – 'was everyone having a good time? Another ice-cream Daniel? Kate, look at the lovely elephant'. The days which always ended with a fight as tearful children were returned to their mother and Dennis returned home to vent his anger and hurt on me.

Not my responsibility? No, it's not a question of duties or rights. My relationship with the children, with Johanna, is my greatest achievement, the hardest thing I have ever done, the source of so much comfort and pride at a time when I feel that everything else in the world has lost all meaning.

We have a friend whose motto is – 'life isn't a dress rehearsal, it's the real thing'. In the last few years of his life Dennis knew that, he sorted out his priorities and for him the real thing was our family – Joey, me, the children. And the newspaper got it wrong.

The paper has always been there. It was the beginning. We met when Dennis Minogue, feature writer, interviewed Bettina Arndt – sexologist? psychologist? for the *Age*. As he wrote in the week before he died – 'The aim was to send her up gutless, she being light relief from the normal task of writing ponderous and pompous pieces on national politics.'

A send-up? More like a proposition, a statement of intent. The *Age* was surprised – where was that famous Minogue objectivity, the cynicism which protects all journalists from themselves? He wrote of 'big, murky, hazel eyes sparkling, mind exploding with enthusiasm. Tina, as bright and bubbling as if talking of romance newly blossomed . . .'

It was a proposition. Within the week Dennis had moved to Sydney, inventing a hundred articles that suddenly had to be written, a hundred interviews with Sydneysiders to grace the pages of a Melbourne newspaper. He was, from the beginning, willing to give up everything; job, home, security, marriage – a marriage which he had presented as over, a civilised living arrangement but which was really far from that. It amazes me now that, knowing the costs, he was willing to risk so much for 'the dawning that comes on me now, my first love, the sweet sixteen come fourteen years late.'

It was far too late. There was never any chance of an innocent romance, of two lovers together locked away from the rest of the world. From the moment we met until his death and now onwards our relationship meant I became part of a network. I met and fell in love with a man but I collected and eventually married a family. There was never a day we were together when I was not reminded that I had a package deal, whether I liked it or not.

We used to joke about my having to accept Dennis, warts and all but in the beginning those warts came close to poisoning any hope we had of a future together.

Even in the days when we weren't allowed to see the children, they were part of our lives. Not just Dennis's sleepless tormented nights but the birthdays, the celebrations with only part of Dennis with me there, the rest was with his children, wondering what they were thinking, whether they were missing their dad.

The Christmas when daddy was given permission to sneak in and deliver the Christmas train set he had spent hours and hours making. Deliver it quickly and then leave before the children returned . . . so as not to upset them with a glimpse of their dad whom they were then supposed to forget.

Then it was mainly Dennis who paid the costs but soon after the load was to shift. Suddenly we were to have the children – every weekend. On Friday night after a week of work, of teaching, of running a business, of travelling, deadlines, decisions, they would arrive and for the next two days I was a stranger in my house, an outsider. Useful for cooking, for picking up clothes, for changing linen when beds were wet in the night, but an embarrassment, a nuisance. When they were there Dennis wouldn't touch me, afraid of making them jealous by showing he cared for me. My pleasure came from watching him glow when they arrived, watching him help them thaw and learn to love him again.

I tried to win my way into their world, by playing mother – a very strange role for me. Making silly birthday cakes, always the second, a day late – the real birthday was always celebrated at home, with their real mummy. I spent each weekend trying to persuade Daniel to let me help him get dressed, do up his buttons. By the end of the weekend he would stop pulling away. The next week he would be back, refrozen – 'Mummy doesn't like you.' Sometimes I would awake to the sound of one of them coughing or crying. I would stumble out to their room. 'Go away, I want Daddy.' And at the end of each weekend they would leave and silence would descend. As I cleaned up the mess I trod on a minefield, trying to choose a careful word, a phrase to help Dennis cope with his depression and anger, the anger which so often turned on me in an attempt to live with the hurt he felt for his children.

Yet the weekends were the best. At least they were part pleasure. In between the endless telephone calls from the woman whose world we had destroyed, the endless fights over money, over who paid for what. The anger and hurt always seemed to revolve over the tiniest of things. I remember so well the note from Johanna attached to the suitcase after I had shrunk one of Daniel's jumpers. 'If you can't wash things properly, don't wash them at all.'

I would end up in a fury over a pair of socks, bought by me and then worn proudly back to mummy's never to appear again.

The irony is that now that I am left with my baby son, I understand so well the overwhelming feelings of hopelessness and dependency that result from six months of broken nights, of giving day and night to a small creature whom only you can comfort. Mother-suckers they call them.

Only now do I have any idea of what it must have been like for Joey. To have been left with not one, but two – to have to cope from day to day, when all you want to do is curl up in a ball and hate the world. The miracle is she was ever able to forgive me.

For everyone reading this who has been there, done that, or who is in the middle of this familiar nightmare, the good news is that we made it. Looking back it is not hard to see when it changed, when it all became easier. I remember well the day Dennis lost his cheer squad, the first time when our fights didn't end up with the three of them against me. I was cooking, and to annoy me Dennis decided to make coffee, pushing me out of the way with a snarl. A bright, young voice intervened; 'Daddy, if you move over a little, Tina could still cook while you make coffee.'

We ended up laughing, and more and more often after this Kate would play the arbiter, telling daddy when he wasn't really being fair to Tina. It really took all the fun out of fighting and now it is a family joke that daddy and I were allowed to fight only because Kate and Dan also squabble sometimes and pick and niggle at each other.

Daniel became easy for me – so like his father – the Irish temper which I had learnt to live with, and the easy forgiveness. I don't think Dan can ever remember his life before me and with him I could remain the tomboy. He loved going to school and telling the news of Tina's wins in Morgan car races, or the time Tina fell out of a tree.

Kate, pretty Kate with her mother's olive skin and chocolate eyes, resented me until I think about a year ago. Used to living with her mother who in some ways is more like a sister, sharing confidences, sitting on the end of her mother's bed while she dressed to go out, living with a couple meant she had to share. She resented us wanting time on our own together, she resented us wanting our own bathroom, sending her back to her own bed after calming her nightmares. She and I used to fight for Dennis's attention – she openly using tears, temper, tantrums as her weapons and I more subtly, finding fault with Kate so she would be less perfect in her father's eyes.

With Kate the breakthrough came with Jesse, the baby boy whose conception we had delayed for year after year until Dennis was sure in his mind that the baby would not harm his children or hurt his wife. When I finally discovered I was pregnant and ran delighted to meet his car in the drive, he told me later his first thought was how to tell Johanna.

Silly, really. Dennis remained so protective of Johanna's feelings even after she and I made peace. Although he used to joke about the horrors of having two wives who compared notes about his worst faults, our new relationship gave him so much pleasure. The day before he died, I now think having some forewarning, he talked to me of the future, what would happen to the children if we were both killed. His solution, which as usual he waited for me to suggest, was for Joey to bring up Jesse with Kate and Dan, his brother and sister. After he died I talked to Joey and found out that weeks before he had talked to her about taking on our son. Typical!

What people don't understand is that it doesn't all end now Dennis isn't here. The network which binds us all together is still there. My mother now talks of inviting Johanna to visit the next time the children stay with her in Canberra. Next week Joey and I are going together to discuss our situation with the private schools which Dennis, not us, felt were so important for his children.

The ironies remain, the petty irritations of living in a world where one in three Australian children live in some sort of single parent or re-marriage situation but where the other two-thirds pretend it isn't happening. One example: medical benefits. In the beginning family cover for Joey, Dennis, Kate, Daniel; separate cover for me. Cheap, easy. We marry – oh well it wasn't worth the trouble, the possible hurt to Joey, Kate and Dan; Jesse, Dennis and me? – a waste of money. So Jesse ended up being added to the family cover and I remained on my own. Joey and I are now thinking of trying to get family cover for us and the three children. Fancy our chances?

It started in the hospital. The people who, not knowing what to say, look around and then seize on my son. 'At least you have your son to comfort you.' 'Jesse will have to stand in for his father.'

Such hollow words. I now feed Jesse in our bed at 4 or 5 am. No longer is there reason to sneak into the living room to give my man his well-deserved sleep. And as Jesse sucks noisily and wriggles and squirms, I cuddle him and hate him for being a small dependent creature instead of my strong man, my rock. I resent his soft red featherdown hair, a poor substitute for his father's woolly red beard, his small silky arms instead of massive chest and bear hugs.

No comfort there, not yet. What was such a blessing to our relationship I know realistically is a sentence to twenty years hard labour. While I revelled in coupledom, domesticity, I now join unwillingly the ranks of the single mothers and I know only too well what is in store.

One Step Away

I drifted, waking each time his small feet wriggled against my thighs, his hot forehead pressed against my arm. The gentle pattern of snort and sniffle which kept me from my sleep failed to irritate. It felt natural, blissful even, this warm cocoon of mother and sick child. The role of comforter was comforting.

The happiness it gave me was touched by guilt. I lay there and thought back to the times my husband had welcomed *his* sick children into our bed and I had lain rigid, annoyed by each cough, each squirm or wriggle. It made me furious that my husband could sleep while his children tossed and turned in *our* bed. Excluded from the bond they shared, I would turn my back and attempt to sleep. And then finally I'd expel the alien presence, persuading my husband to return his child to their bedroom. It hurt him. He didn't understand, couldn't understand.

Now I know the intimacy of sleeping with my own child, and regret denying Dennis that special joy. Sharing a bed with your child is like being with a long-time lover – no strangeness, just familiar skin and smell and breath. It is too late now. Dennis died before I understood the pain I caused him.

Having lived with a man with children I'm aware that the man in my future must buy into similar frustrations. I can only offer a package deal – my child and I together, and I know how difficult this is to accept.

Maybe loving a woman with a child is different from loving a single child. The male role may allow more freedom, more chance to opt in or out of emotional tangles. But I suspect many things are similar. The agony of knowing you can never come first – your lover's time, energy, love must always be parcelled out between the children's and your own needs – and you're second in line. Who would knowingly lay this minefield, which is such a handicap for all future relationships?

The single mother creates for herself a balancing act between the joys and responsibilities of being a parent and her own needs as an adult. She will become the juggler, in every new relationship, keeping the peace, dividing her loyalties – and the tension will be all hers. For the men in her life, once the early fun of playing daddy wears off, three – or even four – will often seem a crowd. For her, the mother, there is no choice. Many of us have the situation thrust upon us – through widowhood or divorce. And we are a growing tribe. The number of one parent families in Australia more than doubled from 130,600 in 1969 to 282,200 in 1981.

Divorce has produced its fair share of these one parent families. Sixty per cent of divorces now involve children. Most of these parents will eventually remarry, starting their new relationships encumbered by the products of the old. We must also consider the increasing numbers of unmarried women who are now choosing to become single mothers. For some it is the preferred choice in facing a difficult decision when dealing with an unwanted, unplanned pregnancy.

Then there are women who deliberately choose to conceive a child to rear on their own. Here it is a planned decision, and the woman concerned will have thought through so many crucial factors – earning capacity, child care, future security, the child's needs. What she cannot know, until it is too late, is just how difficult it is as a mother to form new relationships, to marry and make a marriage work. There's no question – children are a burden on struggling new relationships, a burden which often proves too heavy. As yet there are few Australian statistics but remarriages involving children often don't fare well. Divorce counsellors tell you of the endless strife, the irreconcileable differences that so often divide parent from non-parent, and doom the marriage from the start.

And these are people whose relationships made it to first base, the couples who had enough hope in their future to seek marriage, a permanent commitment. How many others disintegrate far earlier, when the reality of life with children first hits? In many divorces, the children can be the least of the problems. So often marrying a parent means being dragged into a pre-existing network of people, all with their own loyalties, jealousies and quarrels. There are often ex-wives, or ex-husbands, perhaps with their own new partners, and grandparents confused and angry at *their* loss of access. There's money and property – much room for conflict here. Such issues affect even the never-married single mother. Does her new partner take financial responsibility for her children?

There's plenty of cause of strife, but perhaps some of the energy spent quarrelling over these pressures covers an issue more hurtful still – the realisation that, however much he or she tries, the non-parent will always remain a step away from being part of that pre-existing family. It's hard to explain just how painful it can be when you begin to understand that, however much you work to win the affection of the children of your partner, you'll never *really* make it. The parent always has the edge.

It is only now that I have my own child that I can see what that edge is all about. I used to work so hard at pretending to be a mother to my stepchildren . . . cooking favourite meals, making sure there were special treats for lunch packs, creating elaborate birthday cakes. I did so many things their mother would never have bothered to do, things which now, with my own child, I know don't matter.

A friend of mine, a male, once fell in love with a woman with a young child. He told me of his feelings of helplessness and inadequacy when he tried to share the burden of childcare, and found himself so inept. He'd tried to feed the toddler, spoonful after clumsy spoonful until the mother, irritated by watching, would take over. For the parent, a plate of cereal landing in your hair is just part of the daily endurance test . . . it can even raise a smile, sometimes. For the non-parent, the outsider, such moments can so easily represent failure, rejection. And they add up. The real parent shrugs them off. She is boss-cocky. The edge of confidence allows the parent to get away with the tooth fairy who forgets, the favourite toy run over in the driveway, the bad tempers, the broken promises. Children accept much from their parents. The step-parent, mummy's friend, daddy's lover, remains on trial. I remember so well the feeling that at any moment I would blow it, lose my temper, make a wrong move and then in one breath whisk away the tenuous bond that was growing between my step-children and me.

The child caught doing something wrong asks, 'Do you love me, anyway?' Parents don't need to ask, they know. That's what being a parent is all about. For those first few years of your children's life you are given the blessing of unconditional love. Later, when children grow up and look with more critical eyes, you can't be sure of that uncritical acclaim. But in early years, to be a parent is to have power, to revel in the exhilarating knowledge that to that child, you are the one.

It's the heady pleasure of walking into a room filled with people and catching that first flash of joy and recognition in your child's eyes when she or he sees you are there. It's the edge which gives *me* the confidence to leave my child and go to work . . . knowing he's in the hands of a woman with the patience to play Lego for hours on end when I am bored after the first Lego house is erected and smashed. A woman who cooks the scones I can't cook, knits the jumpers he shows off with such pride, lavishes care and endless, endless patience. He'll love me anyway.

A non-parent cannot know the joy of passing it all on, of having a second chance to correct in your child the faults you dislike in yourself, of nurturing in children hidden skills you could have had but lost. The sheer indulgence of parenthood is the hook which makes you susceptible to the most obvious of wiles, makes you too proud one moment, too critical the next. To be a parent is to know excess. You have the right to make the rules and to break them. As a parent I now understand the wicked self-indulgence of the father who allows himself to be cajoled into giving in, who bends the rules because of the pleasure it gives him. As a stepmother I found it so hard to sit back and watch a child manipulate his father into letting him stay up late by snuggling into his lap and saying 'I love you, daddy'. As the outsider, watching, I glowered my disapproval, resenting the fact it was not my lap they sought.

But what if they had chosen me, my lap? That too carried a fear. The fear the natural parent cannot understand . . . the dread of winning the love of someone else's children, forming a bond which is then at the mercy of the vagaries of an adult romance. I talked once to a man who had shared the life of a woman with a child and learnt the joy of being wanted and needed by a tiny tot. Then when, as does happen, the adult relationship changed from love to bitterness, he lost the child he'd taken on as a daughter. No rights, no claims, just resentment from the child's mother that he should feel he'd earned a place in her daughter's life.

The ties in a blended family are easily broken. There's the friend who brought up her stepchildren from toddlers, only to have them reject her totally when they became teenagers filled with adolescent rebellion. (Of course, that sometimes happens in all families, with natural parents as well.) There's the stepfather, whose stepchildren moved to a different country just when he felt he'd become more than a friend. Step-parents run great emotional risks in relationships where they usually have little control. It's in a different league from the tortuous delight of producing your own, monsters though they may be.

And now, with my own son, my experience as both stepmother and mother makes me nervous of imposing my child on another man. It's easier to fight the discipline battles on my own, putting up with his screaming when I refuse a second ice-cream, without a man on the sideline approving my efforts. It's hard enough to tread a middle course between concern and control without eyes watching, picking up my mistakes.

Sometimes I long for someone else's arms to carry the sleeping child from my car instead of having to wake him and watch him stumble ahead as I carry loads of luggage or picnic clutter. Sometimes I long for the firm male voice to say 'no' instead of my pleading he's sometimes learnt to ignore. But what of the times when the man would say 'no' when the mother in me longs to give in? Am I ready for a witness to my indulgences, a judge of my discipline? And in warning other single mothers of the confusion that lies ahead, I wonder if they would be better to enter blind, better not to know.

Postscript

Well, it's happened. Long after writing that original piece, in 1983, I'm to remarry, Jesse will have a new father. The predicted tangle of emotions has already hit and so much of what I'm now experiencing is familiar territory, reminding me of my former life and former marriage.

There is much that is wonderful. The utter pleasure of hearing my son babbling on to other boys about his new daddy, showing him off, making him help catch crabs or make sandcastles, conning him into buying toys or hiring videos. The relief of knowing my boy will grow up like other children, a member of a privileged group of 'normal' families with both a mummy and daddy to appear at school concerts or share the family Christmas.

That's all there, coupled with the unexpected joy of loving again. Peeling back the layers, feeling each other out as we tentatively prepare for the long haul ahead. You are more realistic the second time around, more aware of the hard work of marriage but I am so grateful to be twice blessed – to have had the chance to know and love two very special men.

But the fears are also there. A sadness that this new man in my life, this self-contained bachelor has so little idea of what he is in for as he learns to live with my son. I watch as he tries to cuddle Jesse who responds with a wrestle, already a squirming, embarrassed male shying away from intimacy. I flinch as he stands helpless, trying to cope with a five-year-old's tantrums. I try to stop myself from telling them to be nice to each other, or reprimanding Jesse when he chooses *me* for the bedtime story, instead of his willing new father. They have to forge their own bond and I can only hope that it happens.

Now I'm the go-between, translating, interpreting, loving them both and wanting to bring them close. The fact that I've been there before, on the other side of the fence, simply makes it harder. I laugh at the irony of it all and wish I could spare us the ordeal that lies ahead. But, luckily, I also know that in the end it will be worth it.

Bare Body Comfort

'Bare body confidence.' It was one of those enticing headlines for a frantic pre-summer diet-and-exercise campaign. Let's face it. Bare body confidence I'll never have. But bare body comfort? Well, there I am finally getting somewhere. After years of agony I've acquired a small measure of self-esteem. A few crumbs of confidence which allow me to feel okay about myself, even in circumstances where my very worst warts are revealed for all to see.

It took a long time. I used to flinch at the first touch of a male hand on my flat chest, but I learnt to console myself with the thought that if nothing else (and 'nothing' being the operative word) he would still encounter my playful nipples which loving men taught me to appreciate and enjoy. I'm still not comfortable with top off on the beach, and still wear padded bras to pretend I've more than I do. But I now can very quickly settle into feeling okay, well, sort of okay.

I'm lucky. The good feelings I do have about myself and about my body are all the result of being loved by a man who thought I was great, all over. After seven years of living with someone who ogles and adores whether you are fat or thin, hairy or hungover, you start to believe in yourself. You learn to look into a mirror and even if you don't like what you see, you are able usually to focus on the good things and ignore the bad. There are days when the huge thighs still leap out at you and your stretch marks stand out like neon signs. But you cope. It was a good gift my husband gave me through his blind devotion, and I guard it.

I have to. I suspect my thin veneer of self-confidence will always be somewhat precarious, and easily undermined – particularly by males in my life.

When I first found myself in new relationships after being widowed, it was a surprise to find how quickly I fell back into earlier, self-conscious ways. Clutching the towel around me when walking around the bathroom, lying down flat so my stomach looked smoother. It was a battle not to lose all I had gained.

Quite some time ago I was involved in a long-distance affair – the worst possible relationship for someone like me, who needs time for familiarity to breed comfort. The attraction, as always, was his mind. A clever, talented man, a well-known writer, an academic. But for me there was a major problem . . . his beautiful body. He was a fitness freak, running kilometres every day, working out in the gym – his superb body showed every centimetre run, every gram of sweat lost. I lusted after it but just couldn't handle it. Once, when he was here, I worked hard to get fit and was trimmer than I'd been since a teenager. Foolishly I asked what he thought. He prided himself on his honesty. You could lose three kilos, was the answer. When I stayed with him I found myself sneaking around, waiting until he was out to curl my hair or put on make up. Being with someone who places so much emphasis on looking good made me fall to pieces, my self-esteem in ruins.

Beautiful men aren't for me. I know my limitations. Most of us do. There's research to show we tend to choose partners who have a similar level of attractiveness to ourselves. Ellen Berscheid, a psychologist at the University of Minnesota, showed people photographs of members of the opposite sex and asked them to choose the ones they'd like to meet. The results showed that most people, particularly women, tend to choose to meet partners who look about as good as themselves.

Psychologists have rated the attractiveness of courting couples in bars, theatre lobbies and other public places and found an extraordinary degree of similarity in attractiveness between the dating pair. For 85 per cent of couples, they were not separated by more than one scale point. There was another ingenious experiment in which a selection of wedding photographs were cut up to separate the marrying couples. Then judges were asked to rate the attractiveness of all the individual portraits. Most of the people in the photographs had chosen a partner about as good looking as they were. We stick to our own.

Interesting, isn't it? Most of us obviously feel more comfortable with our own kind. Are we afraid of rejection if we choose a luscious lover? Nervous of keeping up to his or her standards? Maybe we know our egos can't cope if we are hopelessly outclassed.

I have a friend who has suffered all her married life from the knowledge that, as far as her looks are concerned, she married above her station. She's an extremely intelligent, outgoing and vivacious woman who knows she is now considered more attractive as a result of her newly-acquired poise and confidence. It would now be rare for anyone to regard her as less attractive than her husband. Yet when she first married she was constantly aware that her looks were commented on unfavourably compared to her dashing husband. 'People would come up to me and say, "How did *you* catch such a handsome man?" I even heard comments along the lines that he must have married me for money. It was devastating for my confidence and I'm not sure I ever totally recovered.'

The veneer of confidence she has acquired is still very thin indeed. She falls apart at the slightest cutting comment or barbed remark; 'If someone says something about admiring a girl because she's so feminine, I immediately conclude he's trying to tell me I'm *not*. I'm not even sure I *want* to be seen as feminine but I still take it to heart. My antenna is constantly on the alert for a hint of criticism . . . like when someone meets me with one of my children and says "Oh, isn't she pretty. She *does* look like her father!"' Her mother has always been particularly good at the veiled insult, 'Oh, I do like that dress dear, it hides your short neck.' 'Your new haircut is much more flattering. It doesn't accentuate your nose so much.' With that sort of background it's hardly surprising my friend made rather slow progress towards feeling good.

My mother was different. She is a serious woman whose early feminist leanings caused her to reject the preening and pampering traditional to the female character. I grew up being reprimanded for spending too much time in front of mirrors or looking into windows for my reflection. When I started dressing up to go out as a teenager I knew I passed muster if nothing was said. Too much lipstick, too many frills drew sharp comments about looking like a Christmas tree. Some of it has rubbed off, and part of me is able to reject the female devotion to beauty as unnecessary frivolity. Having survived the agonies of adolescence, I now thank my mother for teaching me to place emphasis on more important things . . . I now value the qualities she is so well known for, like caring for other people, being capable, efficient, intelligent, skillful.

After a long separation I'm now living close to an old female friend, a girl I grew up with. Julia has always been a woman who attracted men like flies. I once sat with her in a restaurant in London and at least six males, total strangers, came up to her with totally spurious excuses; 'Weren't you in that film? . . .', 'Haven't I seen you before?'. She brushed them away, casually, carelessly. When we were teenagers together I was the friend invited along for her extra men. I longed to look like her, tried on her dresses, cut my hair the same way. Once I even bought an identical dress, hoping to capture a wisp of her magnetism.

Living apart for the past decade we have had remarkably similar lives, working in similar careers, marrying, raising stepchildren and then each having our own child. She's still breathtakingly beautiful. I could watch her for hours. But I would no longer swap places. At age thirty-four, one of the few things Julia really feels good about is looking good. Her beauty is one of the few areas in which she has total confidence and, funnily enough, it is that beauty which may well have stopped her from gaining confidence in other areas. Her work for instance. Jobs have always fallen into her lap. Her male employers take one look at her and offer her anything, even positions she's not sure she can manage. That's the trouble. She thinks she is competent, a good editor, but so rarely is she employed purely for her talents that she distrusts her own ability. She's been so often admired and pursued that the permanent men in her life have all been winners. Strong, confident men with the self-assurance to come back for more after the initial dismissal, her customary self-defensive brush-off. She's become their prize, to be showed off, admired. In doing so, they have stifled her and undermined her confidence. Winners like their prizes kept in glass cages for all to see. It's too risky to let them loose. 'If you want to be happy for the rest of your life, never make a pretty woman your wife.'

Getting to know her again has made me grateful that I am as I am and look as I look. For me, it was obvious from the beginning that whatever talents I could develop would have to lie in other directions than the physical. It's so much safer to learn to feel good about things you can do, about what you are rather than how you appear. It's an investment which grows with you, with the right nurturing. Beauty is such a dangerous investment and it devalues quickly, often taking too much of your confidence with it.

So there it is. The rationalisation for avoiding hours of tedious beauty care, skipping all but the most obvious of repair jobs. The excuse for cutting corners and ignoring the worst of my defects. I know I'll never now have that boob job I toyed with in my twenties. The wrinkles are beginning to appear, but still I can't resist the beach and can't be bothered to wear a hat. I go to bed with make-up on and refuse to spend fortunes on face packs or anti-wrinkle creams. It's wonderful to be able to say 'no' to the sales-girl who tries to sell me something by dwelling on my defects; 'Don't you think you need something for that dry skin or those blackheads?.' I've come a long way from the time I agonised for days after a tactless beautician asked if I'd ever thought of doing something about my upper lip. Before I'd never even noticed it; but, after that my moustache grew longer and darker each time I looked in the mirror.

Well, these days I'm not so easily disconcerted. I know I can still brush up to look reasonable, wear make-up to camouflage the worst of it, dress to accentuate the good and ignore the bad. Perhaps in ten years I'll feel differently. Maybe it won't be so easy to devalue the physical and pretend I don't mind the veins appearing on the thighs and first signs of the dreaded turkey neck.

Growing old gracefully, that was my plan. Welcoming wrinkles, particularly laugh lines as tributes to a well-lived life. It's so much easier with the comfort of a marriage where the two of us grow old gracefully together. True intimacy is being privy to each other's warts, the disgusting habits you'd reveal only to a loved one. Slopping around the place in the old tracksuit without worrying about spare tires or bumps in the wrong places. Cutting toe nails in the living room, hairy legs all winter, continuing conversations while sitting on the loo.

In my single days I was forced to be on guard to protect self-esteem, to nurture my carefully preserved self-concept. It was back to subterfuge and camouflage, at least until a few barriers came down. There was the constant nerve-wracking threat of being forced at some stage to expose your naked body to the scrutiny of a stranger. It was all a bit of a bore really, and when I staggered out of bed in search of breakfast I'd cast a longing glance at the comfortable, egg-stained dressing gown with broken zip and uneven hem. But I'd look at his sleeping form and think, 'oh no, not yet' and, reaching for the red silk number, make a dash to the bathroom to remove mascara streaks from my cheeks.

Even now, in a new marriage, bare body comfort still eludes me – but I'll get there some day.

Sex, Pregnancy and Motherhood

It amazes me now how little I knew then. When I first started teaching about sex, I was often asked to discuss sex during pregnancy and sex in early motherhood. Talking to medical students, childbirth educators, on radio and television, I quoted from all the right books, reassured women there was no reason why they shouldn't continue to enjoy sexual relations throughout their pregnancies. I gave enthusiastic advice on positions, the beneficial effects of orgasm, lots of do's and very few don'ts. And when asked about afterwards, the afterbirth effects. 'Well,' she said glibly, 'there may be some temporary loss of sexual interest, you may have to wait a little to avoid sexual discomfort, but you'll soon get over it.'

How naive I was. But that was before I had my baby, long before I entered that intoxicating, infuriating state known as motherhood. When I finally took the plunge, I learnt that the textbooks are so often wrong. That, however much you know rationally that sex won't hurt the foetus, emotionally the fear of rocking that very precious boat can be enough to put you off sex for months on end. And that's before – afterwards, when the bombshell of early motherhood first hit, I remember wondering how any woman could possibly entertain erotic thoughts while sleepwalking through the chaos of feeds, nappies, stress and fatigue. I assume my husband and I *must* have had sex at least a few times in that two-year period. Guilt must have motivated me at least that much but I must say I can't remember it happening. Perhaps I dozed through it, who knows.

I can laugh about it now but it makes me annoyed to go back and read the books again and realise how many 'experts' writing books on pregnancy and sexuality are still seeking simple theories to try to explain what must be one of the most complicated, extraordinary experiences a woman will ever have.

Looking at the effects of pregnancy and motherhood on sexuality gives us a superb illustration of the complexity of our sexual response, and just how much it is influenced by everything that makes us human – our personalities, our relationships, our culture, physiological responses and hormones, our past experiences, our emotions, our anatomical shape and size.

Talk to women about what happened to their sexuality during this period of their lives and you will find so many different experiences, influenced by so many different factors. Yet there are still scientists labouring away in laboratories trying to prove post-partum loss of sex drive is due simply to a drop in hormones. There are still obstetricians dismissing a woman's pain during sex as due to post-partum depression.

We are more complicated than that and, unless our individual reactions are taken into account, the experts will continue to be of little help in guiding us through what, for many of us, is a very rocky period in our sexual lives.

But this is a personal story rather than a discussion of research or expert opinion. I want to talk about my experiences during pregnancy and motherhood, not because they are unusual, but because they seem so common. Every time I begin to discuss this topic on a radio programme the switchboard is crammed with women callers, all with their own experiences. Everyone who has been through it has her own story to tell.

To start with the pregnancy. There actually were very good

reasons why Dennis and I should have been particularly neurotic about risks to the foetus. We were both vulnerable. Dennis had lost the first child of his previous marriage, and I had an early miscarriage, a few weeks after discovering I was pregnant for the first time. It wasn't even planned, that first pregnancy. I had gone off the Pill a year before and was patiently awaiting my first post-pill period, but it never came. Instead I noticed I was putting on weight, had funny lumps on my nipples and lo and behold, I was pregnant.

I will never forget the abrupt end to that initial euphoria. Feeling an unaccustomed dampness and looking down in horror to see blood. I've talked to many other women since who have had miscarriages, far later ones involving far more trauma, but we all have that image of blood etched in our minds.

So that started it off – badly. I was eager to be pregnant again and we then experienced a taste of the horror involved in planning sex in order to conceive. It seemed funny at the time – all those years of desperately trying to avoid pregnancies, the heebies of those near misses when the condom broke or we had taken a foolish risk. And now we were trying to make it work and didn't know how. And of course on the crucial nights when you were supposed to do it, everything went wrong. Unexpected visitors arrived, phones rang, you had the flu, the cat went missing, a water main burst. A few months were enough for me. I can't imagine how anyone retains any interest in sex whatsoever when planning for parenthood extends into weeks and months of trying, and every period spells failure.

But, of course, pregnancy wasn't all that was happening in our lives at the time, and our mutual sexual disinterest could have been due to any number of things. Like the fact that we were renovating a house, and so spending romantic evenings knocking plaster off walls and poring over paint pamphlets. Dennis's nights were spent tossing and turning, working out how to pay the bills, mine were equally restless, planning magazine articles for months ahead in case I couldn't work right through the pregnancy.

That's the point no one talks enough about. Sexual desire is affected by everything else that happens in our lives and we almost all go through periods of being over-hassled and sexually uninterested. Luckily, I have always had good friends with whom to share guilty stories about how long it is since the last time we did it. I once had a hilarious time with a girlfriend planning an article on 'How to say no and make *him* feel guilty'. Tut, tut. Not at all the way a sexologist is supposed to behave!

There were other funny things about pregnancy, for me at least. Like body image. Here I was having spent a lifetime with no boobs and now I was sporting this perfectly respectable pair of knockers. Well, I suppose 'knockers' is a bit of an exaggeration, but there was this one wonderful moment when I woke up in hospital within a few days of Jesse being born and my milk just 'came in', as they say. There I was, sitting up proud as Punch with these huge, bursting breasts. It was the most extraordinary sensation.

But large breasts, which to me had always epitomised female sexuality, didn't make me feel any sexier. I felt . . . well 'womanly', I suppose. This was a strange sensation and was due at least in part to the way men treated me. No longer was I whistled at, or ogled or flirted with. I was treated like Mother Earth – with respect, and a nice, wholesome concern. It was all very nice, but it certainly doesn't do much to make you feel like a desirable vamp.

Talking to other women about this, many have told me they suddenly became aware of how much their image of themselves as sexual people was dependent on feedback from males . . . the wolf whistles, blatant undressing stares. Those things which we may well find offensive but still help build up our sexual confidence. To lose this male sexual attention can be devastating for the woman who hasn't learned to believe in her own desirability. I was lucky. As an older mum, I think such things had less effect on my sexuality than they would have done when I was younger. I could cope with the odd stretch marks and slightly flabbier tummy.

Yet when I was working as a therapist I can remember sitting with delicious-looking twenty-two-year-olds who were so upset at the slight changes that had occurred to their previously perfect figures. Young women who had previously been quite uninhibited about parading naked in front of their husbands found themselves clutching for towels or dimming the lights. One girl found she could no longer climax in her favourite on-top position because she was so self-conscious about her flabby breasts being exposed to her husband's view. It was a shame, for both of them, because her new self-consciousness stopped her enjoying the breast fondling that had previously contributed so much to her excitement.

Pregnancy produces physical changes in our bodies which thrust us headlong into womanhood, and I feel our reaction to these changes depends on how much we are indoctrinated into the youth culture, how much we are able to welcome the aging process or want to fight to remain young.

I remember feeling very ambivalent about the changes I noticed in my nipples, changes which increased during pregnancy and remained from then on. I lost the small, light pink areolas that symbolise adolescence and young womanhood. I found myself staring in amazement at my large dark nipples. It was weird, and reminded me of photographs in *National Geographic* magazine of African women with eager babies suckling greedily at immense, extended breasts.

Late in my pregnancy I was learning pushing out exercises for the pelvic muscles and, following my child-birth educator's advice, I put a hand mirror between my legs to watch what was happening. What I saw was a shock. Gone were the light-pink lips tucked neatly in folds to discretely cover the vaginal opening. Instead, there was large, dark-red and swollen tissue bulging outwards as if at the peak of prolonged sexual excitement, opening like bulging petals to reveal maroon, even purple vaginal walls. That wasn't me. That blatant, bulging, blossoming creature was nothing like the woman I had been.

In case you are wondering, for most women the genitals *do* resume something like their former colour and shape, although the vaginal lips may always remain a little darker. Yet, at the back of my mind there is always the thought that I don't look the same and perhaps that I don't look or feel as nice. It is hard to not feel that males constantly long for pink near-virgins rather than the riper older woman. How many women, like me, after giving birth find themselves wondering if they still feel the same to him? Can a man tell if you have had a vaginal delivery? Are you perhaps less snug, less stimulating? After you have experienced the incredible stretching as the baby's head forces its way through, it is hard to image that your vagina could ever recover.

Of course, if you do your vaginal exercises, after a while you usually end up with a vagina much the same as it was before, but it's one of the things which makes those first few times after the birth rather worrying. There is also the fear that sex will hurt – hardly surprising when you consider how many women spend the few weeks after the birth hobbling around like horsemen after a rough ride. It's partly due to stitches, repair operations following an episiotomy. Episiotomies (a surgical incision in the perineum at the rear of the vagina) are one of the more controversial childbirth practices. Many experts in natural childbirth are now producing evidence that episiotomies are far more common than is necessary, and are a classic example of an increasing medical interference in the birth process. There is no doubt that some nervous obstetricians prefer to routinely use episiotomies rather than acquire the skills necessary to simply monitor the natural stretching of the vaginal opening. What is worse, often the obstetrician will not take sufficient care in performing the repair after the episiotomy, leaving women with permanent, painful scaring around the vaginal opening.

Sometimes an episiotomy *will* be necessary to avoid tearing at the vaginal entrance, but it's important to choose an obstetrician willing to treat the genitals with the care they deserve, and choose the course *least* likely to lead to discomfort and possible permanent scaring. I vividly remember watching other women in hospital with me who, long after my own stitches had painlessly disappeared, were still virtually crippled by their tender vaginas.

What fascinates me is the fact that there are women who seem to have none of these fears, and who can't wait to leap into having intercourse within days of giving birth. I once spoke to a woman whose husband used to sneak into the hospital ward late at night and draw the curtains for a mutually enjoyable quick romp, surrounded by a ward full of nursing mums. Sex was the furthest thing from my mind at that time as I was submerged in new experiences . . . learning to breastfeed, sitting up in the middle of the night talking to other mothers, learning to put on nappies. I'd also had a few stitches, which didn't exactly make me eager to leap into having intercourse – going to the loo for the first time was enough of a shock!

Then, once you are home, you are thrown in at the deep end – trying to fit in all your chores between the hours and hours of feeding, changing, nursing and blissful gloating over your wonderful new creation. I was lucky enough to have a good baby who did most of the right things at the right times. But even then I stumbled through in a haze of exhaustion, sleeping fitfully, waiting for the first cry, and feeling constantly tense about whether I was behaving as a good mother should.

What amazes me is that anyone ever expects women to recover their sex drive in these circumstances. It's also a time when your relationship with your husband or partner must go through one hell of a readjustment. It must be very hard for a man not to feel some jealousy or resentment at having to compete for attention with such a demanding little creature. It's not easy to make early parenthood a shared experience. Even if you are not breastfeeding, it's difficult for the father to feel as close to his child as you do, or to acquire the same nurturing skills. I remember one morning leaving Jesse asleep with his father to care for him while I raced off to do some shopping. I returned home to a bawling baby and a furious father, quite wrung out with frustration at trying to comfort a perverse creature who wanted his feed two hours early. The strain must be there in even the best of relationships – one more burden on a shaky sex drive, or what's left of it.

In these circumstances it is hard not to feel guilty about depriving your man. You sink into bed, desperate for sleep and lie there feeling that eager penis in the small of your back, those tentative hands exploring to see if you are interested. And all you want is to snatch some precious moments when no one wants anything from you. How awful it is when your patient husband becomes just one more demand, one more person asking something of you.

I know there are hormonal changes which occur after pregnancy which could account for some of the loss of libido most women experience during early motherhood. The hormones are known to produce less lubrication, decreased enjoyment and libido. But for me, it seems crazy to isolate these physical changes from the immense emotional upheaval you experience when you first become a mother and the effects on your relationship. Having been through it, it really doesn't surprise me that many women take a long time to recover from the shock. It's years before some women's sex drive re-emerges, and they find themselves enjoying sex once again. I think part of the problem is that often you start having sex because you feel guilty about constantly knocking your husband back, but you would really prefer to be asleep! In these circumstances it's hardly surprising that you don't respond. If you keep on doing this and having sex when you aren't in the mood, you stop looking forward to the next time – sex becomes a chore, one more thing to get over with.

From the male point of view it's pretty obvious you're only doing it to please him. He resents that and starts to niggle you about it . . . and so it goes on. It can be very difficult for a relationship to survive these pressures. If it does, it's a fair sign that you have the sort of communication which will get you through whatever troubles lie ahead.

And then, finally, you may begin to see some sexual bonuses from having survived the experience of becoming a mother. I've spoken to many women who feel they blossomed sexually only after becoming mothers. It's hard to tell why this should be. Certainly the physiological changes that occur during pregnancy could help arousal by increasing blood flow in the genital tissues. Perhaps you are just that much older, wiser and in tune with your body. For many women there *is* a link between the experience of giving birth and the experience of orgasm. I'm aware of that now, although I found nothing sensuous about giving birth. There was something exhilarating about working to control the pain and struggling to keep on top of it, but sexual, never! Yet now, during orgasm, I sometimes have flashbacks to giving birth. There's a special type of orgasm in which my uterus contracts and vagina pushes out just like final stage of labour. It's a glorious sensation and something I've only felt since having a baby.

So I'm one of the lucky ones. My bumpy sexual road has smoothed out and I look back on those sexually barren years with amazement. Yet perhaps it is natural that the energy required to cope with procreation should temporarily diminish the recreational aspects of sex. Many of us do seem to need time out from our normal sexual drive to learn to become mothers. I wouldn't have missed the experience – whatever the effects on my sex life. But it sure is nice to come out the other end, brush off the cobwebs and rediscover lust. It's amazing how quickly the rust disappears.

New Roles, New Rules

New Rules, Old Expectations

'Women hope men will change after marriage but they don't; men hope women won't change but they do.'

It's an interesting thought, isn't it? It intrigued me and pondering on it led to 'Men and Marriage', a look at how men are reacting to the changes which are taking place in our assumptions about marriage. It was written for men, about men, as part of a very deliberate attempt to persuade males to start thinking about some of the issues which are affecting *their* personal lives.

It's a real growth industry as far as psychological research is concerned. After focussing so long on women's issues, researchers are now increasingly looking at how some of the shifts in female expectations about their roles are affecting men. But it's not so easy to persuade men, or the publishers of magazines read predominantly by males, that men are interested in such 'soft' issues. That says it all, doesn't it? Men are supposed to be concerned with 'hard' news, while 'soft' issues like health, relationships and social issues are lumped on to the women's pages or left for daytime television.

Well, it's finally changing, and my experience has been that many men are keen to learn more about personal relationships, health and social issues, and increasingly resent the notion that such concerns are out of their domain. Perhaps the greatest reaction I've had to an article written for men was 'The Devastation of Divorce', when male after male talked to me about their personal reactions to divorce. There is overwhelming evidence that males are confused by the changes which have occurred in male and female roles, and feel extremely isolated by having so few opportunities for discussing their feelings.

But men aren't the only ones caught between new rules and old expectations. Women, too, are doing their share of navel-gazing as they try to balance out the increasing demands of careers with their traditional roles as wives and mothers. The articles included in this section – on single women, superwomen, on workaholics – give only a glimpse of some aspects of the new lives of women. And yes, I know they focus mainly on the positive – the *advantages* of being a superwoman, the women who *choose* to remain single, the *contented* workaholics. It's a distortion which ignores the very real problems still plaguing the lives of many women – the increasing numbers of women struggling to support children on their own, single mothers, deserted wives, the women forced to work in dreary, underpaid jobs, the women stuck in relationships with violent men.

But having lived and worked through a period which brought great change to the lives of women, I marvel at the improvements. I have watched my friends, the women I have seen as clients or meet through my work. Watched as their lives expanded, as they faced new options, new risks in their careers, and in their relationships. These women have had so much more freedom than our mothers did . . . and they have made the most of it. They are the lucky ones – but surely it's worth rejoicing that for some the choices are there.

Men and Marriage

The married man had it made. Despite all the jokes about nooses and henpecked husbands, the traditional marriage provided the male with one of life's great deals – in return for his services as breadwinner and provider he received respect, care, emotional support plus that most invaluable of assets – someone to find his lost socks. He was the decision-maker, lord of his domain, she chief bottle-washer, sock-finder, and emotional hub of the family.

He loved it. All the recent evidence shows that marriage provided the male with a haven of safety and contentment. Men simply don't cope very well on their own. Their health suffers, their happiness suffers. And they know it. Even once-bitten men are eager to try again, rather than risk remaining single. Divorced men in Australia take a quick look (an average of four years) at the life of singles and then rush headlong back into remarriage. They know what's good for them. Divorced men die more frequently from road accidents, suicide and alcoholism than married men. British research shows single men are twice as likely to kill themselves as married males of the same age, four times as likely to enter a mental hospital, more likely to suffer a coronary or die of some form of cancer. In the United States the mortality rate is two to three times higher amongst separated and divorced men from practically any major disease – lung cancer, tuberculosis, coronary diseases – than it is among the successfully married. Research from the University of Colorado showed separated and divorced American males are nine times more likely to be admitted to a psychiatric hospital than are married men. In Australia the effects of marriage on male health and happiness have not received the same scrutiny, but what evidence there is points in the same direction. A 1979 survey by the Health Commission of NSW showed that married men experienced fewer 'psychological problems' such as heavy drinking, stress, emotional problems, depression, dissatisfaction with careers than the unmarried males. The Families in Australia study by the Family Research Unit at the University of NSW showed divorced males are two-and-a-half times more likely than married men to be receiving mental health treatment.

That's the male side of the story. But when we look at the welfare of wives, there emerges a different picture. In the early 1970s, American sociologist Jessie Bernard wrote *The Future of Marriage* (Bartam, New York, 1973) in which she distinguished between the husband's marriage and the wife's marriage, providing evidence to show that, 'being married was only half as good for wives as for husbands, not only in terms of survival, but in other terms as well'. Whereas for the husband, marriage reduced the chance of premature death through disease or suicide, and protected men from mental illness and psychological distress, for wives, marriage proved a health hazard. More married women than married men show phobic reactions, or depression, symptoms of psychological distress and mental health impairment.

Married women in Australia have shown similar signs of wear and tear. The Families in Australia study showed that more married men than married women report good mental health. Excluding sufferers of alcoholism and mental retardation, figures show more married women than men are admitted to Australian psychiatric institutions. Twice as many Australian women as men take unprescribed drugs such as aspirin, daily, – primarily for nerves and tension headaches. Twice as many women as men are prescribed barbiturates and psychotropic drugs used for 'treatment' of psychological disturbances of one sort or another. A 1971 report from a Melbourne hospital showed females attempt suicide twice as frequently as males.

It may be that some of these apparent differences in health and happiness of married men and women are due to cultural factors which make it easier for a woman to admit to suffering emotional problems and to seek medical assistance. 'A cup of tea, a Bex and a good lie down' – female solutions to emotional complaints to which the true Aussie bloke would be loath to admit. Yet a comparison of the married women with her single sisters reveals it is marriage rather than femaleness which endangers her health and happiness. A 1971 study of community health in Canberra showed single women had only two-thirds the rate of mental health disturbances of married women. Overseas research shows single women show greater happiness, fewer neurotic tendencies, less depression and are less likely to end up in mental hospitals than married women of the same age.

The message was clear. His marriage, the male-dominated institution that contributed so much to his well-being, was all too often at the expense of hers. Marriage protected husbands but endangered wives. But marriage is changing. The Australian woman is changing, moving out of her traditional role as wife and mother.

And, as her life expands to encompass other roles, the married woman moves up in the happiness stakes. She gains new self-esteem, confidence; her marriage is a better deal. But the sands are shifting beneath *him*.

Talking to men about marriage these days you'll find there's often a note of wistfulness, a yearning for days gone by. They look back to their parents' marriages, the days when men were men and women knew their place, and everything seemed so much easier. It's obviously true that it was so partly because we didn't have the same high, 'unrealistic' expectations of marriage, there was less navel-gazing, more commitment to what was seen as the normal hard work of married life. Even when people were unhappy, they were less likely to talk about it, more ready to accept their lot.

For men who entered marriage with the same expectations, it's a shock to find the rules have changed. Who can blame them for resenting the shift? As the saying goes; 'Women hope men will change after marriage but they don't, men hope women won't change but they do.'

The attitudes of Australian women toward marriage *are* changing dramatically. Helen Glezer, of the Institute of Family Studies in Melbourne, found that the attitude of women to the roles partners should play in marriage had shifted significantly between 1971 and 1982. Comparing data gathered from two groups of eighteen to thirty-four-year-olds, a decade apart, Glezer found that women no longer believed husbands should be the sole providers.

In 1971, a majority (72 per cent) of women felt that 'wives who don't have to work should not do so'. By 1982, only 46 per cent agreed with that. Women no longer believe that men should rule the roost. In 1971, 44 per cent believed that 'important decisions should be made by the husbands'. The figure had dropped to 16 per cent by 1982.

Even more dramatic is the changing view of motherhood. Support for the notion that women are only fulfilled through motherhood dropped from 68 per cent in 1971 to 30 in 1982. Women no longer regard motherhood as their most important role. In 1971, 78 per cent rated motherhood as their *raison d'etre*; by 1982, only 46 per cent gave it such a high priority.

Young (eighteen to thirty-four) married men confronted by the same questions appeared at first to be models of egalitarianism, showing little difference from the female in many of their attitudes. Most of them felt that motherhood was not necessarily the most important fulfilling aspect of a woman's life, most felt that husbands should help with housework.

The same men were somewhat less comfortable with the idea of women working who did not need to do so – many were not so keen on giving up their role of being the primary breadwinner. Nor were they quite so willing to acknowledge a shift in power in the family decision-making – only 16 per cent of the women in the 1982 sample felt that important decisions should be made by the husband, compared to 29 per cent of the males.

Plenty of men still intend to go down fighting, clinging to a traditional view of marriage roles. The Family Research Unit found that, in every age group under sixty, more men than women supported male-dominated marriage roles. Men were more likely to believe the father should have final say in important family decisions, that a mother should always support the father in the family if the children criticised him, that a husband should be older than his wife and so on.

Changes in attitudes are most likely to occur in the higher socio-economic groups. Glezer has shown that working-class husbands and wives – in particular, those of non-English-speaking backgrounds with non-working wives – are the more likely to express traditional views. With less power over their lives, less chance of finding other sources of emotional satisfaction, it makes sense for the less advantaged to cling to marital roles which provide emotional security – particularly in times of economic recession.

Even among women returning to the workforce, the main motivation of a substantial proportion is extra income – they work out of economic necessity, rather than desire.

In August 1984, the Clemenger advertising company published a survey on Australian women which found that of a total of 39 per cent in the workforce, 25 per cent claimed their work was income orientated. Fourteen per cent of the women were 'career' orientated – they claimed they worked for enjoyment, independence or to further their careers. Of the remaining 61 per cent of women presently not in the workforce a further 17 per cent intend to work – 62 per cent of this group have children under five years of age – and many are currently seeking employment. Yet many of these women who start off working mainly for economic reasons find their attitudes change. As one mother said in the survey; 'It starts off, you need the money, and so you go back to work, and then you find you enjoy it because it gets you out of the house.' And another had this to say; 'I really love my job.

I think I would be lost if I was retrenched. I think I would die of loneliness.'

Many women are learning that it wasn't marriage that made them unhappy, rather it was the restrictions and the isolation of their roles as housewife and mother. The unhappiest group of women in the Clemenger study were the young women at home with young children who were intending to go back to work. Compared to other groups these women were found to be more dissatisfied with life in general, their achievements, their social standing in the community.

A 1981 study by the University of Melbourne looked at the life satisfaction and well-being of Australian men and women, and found that married women were conspicuously less satisfied than single people or married men. When they divided the married women into categories such as working women, older women whose children have left home, young mothers etc., it was only the women at home with children who were 'manifestly dissatisfied'. Working women reported higher 'well-being' scores and higher satisfaction with all sorts of aspects of their lives than housewives.

Naturally the more women join the workforce, the more difficult it becomes for other women to feel satisfied in roles which no longer are accepted as the norm. So the drift continues and while working increases married women's happiness, in the short term at least, it appears to be undermining the long-established happiness of their mates.

There's tension, and in many marriages the uncertainty about changing roles: his concern about loss of status and power, her concerns about juggling her roles as wife, mother and working woman, are sometimes played out over the most trivial of issues – his inability to find his own socks, disputes over who should wield the tea towel, or remember to buy the toilet paper or pick up the drycleaning on the way home from work. Like the divorcing couple fighting over custody of the goldfish, these skirmishes on the domestic front are merely surface bubbles of underlying ferment of changing roles. Remember these young males in Helen Glezer's study so ready to voice their support for equal marital roles, mutual sharing and caring? – Well, when it comes to the nitty-gritty of marital life, the reality is rather different. Many of these 'chauvinists in sheep's clothing', as one woman unkindly called them, aren't really so keen on equality when actually faced with a pile of dirty clothes, or a fridge that needs defrosting. Helen Glezer found that when the couples were asked who actually performed domestic tasks, most working women are still carrying the brunt of domestic chores.

Even the 'good' husbands, the helpful husbands, usually wait to be asked. 'Can I help you, dear?' They are eager to lessen her load, but the load is still *hers*. The working wife is left with constant distraction of a mind overflowing with the trivia of running a household, of having to ask for help and being grateful, and even in the best of marriages, sharing everything but the guilt. She's the one who feels guilty if she works late. She is the one who feels guilty if their son baulks at the baby sitter or runs away from school. She's the one who feels guilty if her train is cancelled due to a rail strike – he's at home already preparing dinner . . . and waiting to be thanked.

What has happened, here and overseas, is that while more working women are now sharing economic responsibilities with their husbands, on the domestic front they are still on their own. (If it's any consolation, it's not just the Aussie bloke who is avoiding the bucket and squeegy. The American working wife spends an average of 26 hours a week on housework. Her husband spends 36 minutes. In Denmark, husbands spend 1¾ hours compared to their working wives' 21 hours. The British *Sunday Times* found only 2 per cent of British men take any part in British housework.

Studies of the division of domestic labour have produced all sorts of fascinating facts – as women have more children, the husband's participation in childcare tends to diminish – the novelty wears off; as women move from part-time to full-time work, the husband's contribution changes very little, it is hers which falls off. No, it's not usually that she pays others to do it for her – it's a case of cutting corners. It's easy to ignore green mould in the back of refrigerators when you aren't home to watch it grow.

Helen Glezer found bickering over housework was the number one area of conflict in her marital study. The battles over the kitchen sink reflect the uncertainty both men and women still feel about women's right to choose to do more than tend to the fire and nurture the caveman when he returns to the fold. It's bad enough that we are not there waiting to hear his tales of fighting the bears – let alone shoving a tea towel into his hand as he enters the cave. The husband's unwillingness to share responsibility for running the home and caring for the children constantly undermines the wife's right to work and denies any possibility of an equal partnership. So she struggles to fulfill her role as wife and mother on top of her outside work to absolve her guilt at wanting some escape from her family responsibilities.

Amidst all the confusion, the bottom line in all the arguments is the difficulty women experience in communicating with their husbands about their needs and the apparent inability of many men to try to genuinely understand, to listen and talk about their feelings. 'The word,' Thomas Mann wrote, 'Even the most contradictory word, preserves contact – it is silence which isolates.' There obviously *are* reasons why men find it difficult to share the household chores – the threat to their manhood, fear of ridicule from other men, uncertainty about performing tasks where they have few skills and are ridiculed when they appear incompetent. How many women undermine male confidence by constantly taking over, 'Here, let me do that,' she says as he struggles to put on the nappy, or joking at the dinner party about Fred turning the washing pink.

Many women are reluctant to allow men to enter *their* domain. They don't want men to acquire skills in what has traditionally been their area of competence and one of their main sources of self-esteem. So while they complain about the male's unwillingness to share in domestic duties, they continually push the male out when he moves too far and too confidently into what has previously been their exclusive world.

So while the female may have her own struggle with relinquishing and sharing roles, often her real beef is not about his attitudes but his inability to discuss them. A British survey of marital satisfaction of 10,000 women conducted by Dr Robert Chester of Hull University found that most were satisfied with their husbands as breadwinners and supporters, but up to one-third complained their partners were inept as companions and ineffectual as confidants.

Traditionally, marriage involved a kind of bartering, rather than mutual inter-dependence or role-sharing. Husbands financially and economically supported wives, while wives emotionally, psychologically and socially supported husbands. He brought home the bacon, she cooked it. He fixed the plumbing, she the psyche. Along with the shift in economic balance in the family, women are now beginning to resent their continuing emotional support of men and are expecting men to supply the same emotional input into relationships as they do. The trouble is that most of the men they are reaching out to have been reared in emotional straight-jackets where it is considered unmanly not only to talk about inner emotions but even to be aware of them. Males are simply not skilled at the art of 'examining one's innards', the soul-baring talk which is the essence of intimacy for many women.

More important than sharing the dishes, women seek to *connect* with their partners rather than simply providing emotional servicing for a tight-lipped tower of strength. Research shows males are poor at noticing non-verbal signals from others, and apparently are especially insensitive to signals from a partner with whom they are not getting on. Marriage guidance counsellors report that males are often unaware of the signs of impending marriage break-up until it is too late. Then they are left wondering what hit them.

A study by Brisbane-based counsellor at the Family Court, Peter

Jordan, shows that in Australia at present the decision to separate is largely made by women. It is women who are walking out and divorcing their husbands. Australian women aren't the only ones – 75 per cent of divorces in the United States are initiated by women and for every man in Britain who divorces his wife, three women divorce their husbands.

Deprived of emotional support, the divorced man fares very badly indeed. He is often totally bewildered at finding himself rejected for failing to provide his marriage partner with services he never considered part of the marriage contract, 'My wife abandoned me for absolutely no reason whatsoever . . . I was a good husband . . . a good provider.'

The rules of the game have changed. A successful marriage today depends on skills like communication, sensitivity and intimacy, which are alien to many men but the lifeblood of most women. Women's new-found economic independence has changed the balance of power in many relationships. Now she is making the rules and when he doesn't know how to play, she's the one who calls for the umpire – he retires hurt. In the short term, at least, the neanderthal man hankering after his lost club is in for trouble. But there are plenty of other men hanging in there, battling their way through unfamiliar emotional jungles and discovering in the process that the two-way street of modern marriage has a lot going for it – a happier wife can even make up for the constant threat of dishpan hands.

The Devastation of Divorce

'Total devastation'; 'like being hit on the head by a piece of four-by-two'; 'falling apart'; 'shattered' . . . These are emotional phrases used by Australian men to describe an event which has destroyed their personal world – divorce.

A report released by the Family Court of Australia contains research showing the crippling effects of divorce and separation on men's emotional and physical health. It contains the first published local research focussing exclusively on male reaction to divorce and confirms overseas evidence of men's vulnerability in the breakdown of a marriage.

In a world where men are often seen as controlled, unemotional decision-makers, the results of this important research holds some surprises:

■ In Australia it is women rather than men who are making the decision to end the marriage. In 65 per cent of cases studied, the wife made the decision to separate (the husband's decision accounted for 19 per cent of divorces and 16 per cent involved mutual agreement).

■ Upon separation most men experience emotional and physical symptoms normally associated with extreme grief or stress. Most report crying, sleeplessness, extreme tiredness, loss of energy and appetite. They have difficulty concentrating at work and coping with newly acquired domestic responsibilities and often suffer loneliness and social isolation.

■ It is usually the man who attempts reconciliation after the separation. More than half the men studied made some attempt at reconciliation but only 7 per cent of the wives. Most often the wife rejects the attempt to resuscitate the marriage.

■ Up to two years after the divorce most men are still feeling they have been dumped by their wives; a third feel the divorce was a horrible mistake and over a third feel they will never get over the breakup of their marriage.

■ Almost a quarter of the men still do not know what went wrong and why the marriage ended.

Peter Jordan, a Family Court counsellor in Brisbane, decided to conduct research into the effects of divorce on men after counselling his first twenty-one males involved in separation proceedings and discovering that twenty of them were bewildered, angry and often in tears. 'I was surprised because I expected the women to be the ones who were distressed. Here were these men desperately wanting the marriage to continue, pleading, crying, offering anything, promising anything to persuade their wives to come back. I thought: "What is going on here?" and went looking for research on male reactions to divorce and found very little had been done.'

Jordan found men were often frightened by their extreme reactions to the divorce and horrified to find themselves breaking down; 'Men often use the term "breaking down" as if they are machines coming to pieces. We mainly use the expression in relation to men . . . for instance when Kim Hughes shed a few tears at his press conference he was reported as breaking down. Our community seems to feel if men show emotion they are in danger of permanently falling apart – and the men themselves fear that is what's happening and are frightened by it.'

Men who had been separated for between one and two years were contacted through the court's Brisbane registry and asked to fill in a questionnaire examining their experiences. One hundred and sixty-eight men took part in the study. Most were in their late twenties and thirties, born in Australia and working full-time in white collar (41 per cent) and blue collar (49 per cent) occupations.

Jordan found ample evidence of the stress he had encountered in counselling divorced men, with 60–80 per cent of the men reporting long lasting stress-related symptoms such as sleeplessness, crying, reduced energy, poor appetite and excessive tiredness.

The men most likely to fall apart were those who did not want the marriage to end and whose wives unexpectedly left them. The men who coped best had instigated the separation. This finding supported overseas research showing that the spouse initiating the divorce may experience greater stress prior to separation and a later guilt reaction but it is the non-initiating spouse who is more likely to suffer feelings of rejection, anger and resentment at the time of separation.

Since, in Australia, the wives are deciding to leave, it is not surprising to find that, in the main, husbands are suffering.

For many men, it is only when the marriage ends that they realise the extent and intensity of their attachment to their marriage, wife and children. The man is often confused to discover the depth of his feelings and searches blindly for an explanation.

David is a thirty-nine-year-old doctor, now a single father looking after his three children. After over a decade of marriage, he and his ex-wife drifted apart. He says; 'She stopped loving before I did. I sensed it but only realised it afterwards – body language they call it. I do not think she wanted it to happen that way. But, in the end, I reckoned she gave up trying to deny what was going on and fell in love with someone else and wanted to marry him.

He lived in another country and had no money to support our children so she had to make a choice – me and the children or him and a new start. By then, I had lost that sixth sense of her emotions and she became foreign to me. We finished up sitting on opposite sides of the room intellectually sparring the pros and cons of the options. There seemed little to choose from. I became a single parent. She went away. I did not understand. Then came my emotion; the stunning disbelief of what was happening. Was I just watching a mid-afternoon soap opera? Perhaps if I turned off the TV, it would all go back to normal. I began to experience what I had been taught and had read about. I wept savagely for the relationship; for me. I was angry at the world for being such a rotten place. I desperately wanted to know why it was happening to me. I was angry with my parents for having made me an emotional cripple and too much for her to live with.

'It really was very simple, I reasoned in my head. She was a person with every right to seek happiness. It was too bad that it was not me she wanted but soon I will find someone else as she has. Sure, we had grown apart, stopped communicating, whatever those clichés mean. The turmoil made me sick. The self-hate ruined my appetite and sleep. The ghost of the relationship lived on in the inanimate objects around me. I wanted to run away but felt trapped by three needy souls. I wanted to be alone but felt lonely. The same rotten unanswerable questions kept coming up over and over. Was I really that bad to live with? What was wrong with me or was it her?'

Why? Was it her or me? Jordan's research shows that many men – even two years after the divorce – are left wondering about this. Twenty-six per cent did not know why their wives wanted the marriage to end. Most husbands felt that it was their wives' attitudes, feelings and personalities which was the main cause of the marriage breakup.

Yet when Jordan asked about serious sources of conflict in the relationship, the couples fought most over finance and the husbands' work.

Jordan says; 'There is often a difference between the husband's perception of what was going on and the real sources of conflict. I remember one couple where the reason she married him was she valued him as a companion and enjoyed their close, supportive relationship. Then soon after they married he took a job which kept him away from home six months of the year. He felt he was taking the job for the sake of the family, she felt she had lost the very thing she had married him for. The problem was they had no mechanism for communicating how they both felt; she tried but he didn't know how to listen.'

Increasingly, couples are finding a disparity between the man's expectations regarding his role as breadwinner/provider and the attitude of his wife. Women are moving away from the traditional view that the man's most important contribution to marriage is to go out into the world, work and provide for the family.

As women join the workforce and contribute financially to the marriage, they seek more companionship from their partners, active involvement in raising the children and sharing domestic responsibilities. They question whether their husbands' complete commitment to work has more to do with competitiveness and 'workaholism' than any real material need.

Many men are unable to work out what their wives want. But it is not as if their wives are not trying to tell them. Jordan finds out that often the woman has spent months or years trying to communicate with her husband about what's happening to their relationship, often long before she considers separation.

All too often the husband dismisses her complaints as female whingeing. Says Jordan; 'Men tend to dismiss their wives' complaints . . . "She's just feeling off-colour"; "Just a bit uptight, you know what women are like . . . that time of the month"; they expect women to be emotional and get upset over matters they regard as unimportant, so they just tune out. It all just washes over their heads.'

So the husband does not hear what the woman's trying to say and at a certain point she moves towards the decision to end her marriage. Sometimes she may have an affair – an event which is often seen as a cause of the marriage breakdown but may in fact be a symptom of a marriage being in trouble. Research on affairs shows women usually have extra-marital relationships when their marriages are not providing the emotional satisfactions they seek.

And what of that classic divorce scenario of the middle-aged man seeking a retread for his well-worn type? There is no doubt it is still happening, just as there are couples who simply drift apart or who know from the start that it is all a ghastly mistake. But most divorces are taking place not towards the end nor at the beginning but somewhere in the restless middle of her marriage rather than his.

Often the woman goes through her grieving for the marriage long before she actually leaves. By the time her decision is public the couple are at different stages in terms of their acceptance of the breakdown. His grief commences long after hers has been and gone. She has to watch wild displays of emotion, pleas to seek counselling, to talk, to communicate from the man she has hammered at for years to open up and talk to her. It is too late.

As a counsellor, Jordan struggles to help men understand; 'The men can't understand how she can just sit there and say: "Why don't you wake up to yourself – it's been over for a year. Why are you crying now?" She's at the stage of moving on, looking ahead to a new life and he's just been hit by a sledge hammer. He can't understand why she seems so cold and composed when his world is shattered.'

Peter Jordan's research showed that before separation many men are unaware of their wife's thoughts about their relationship. It does not occur to them that she could be thinking of leaving and when told, they sometimes choose not to hear.

As Jordan points out, many men are not aware of the precarious nature of their marriage because they choose not to be involved in the emotional and everyday happenings in their home; 'The responsibility for the emotional stability of a marriage is placed in the woman's hands very early in their relationship. It is not uncommon to hear men commenting: "A woman's place is in the home and she is responsible for that area," or "My role

is to go to work and bring in the money." When responsibility
for nurturing and maintaining the relationship is given to the wife,
with it also goes the power to end the relationship. The consequence for many men, therefore, is that having given their wives
the power (consciously or unconsciously) in the marriage such
power can be used against them. Many men being unaware of
the power and responsibility their wives have, are shocked at separation. Such men feel let down by someone they trusted with their
marriage, and so they believe and feel it has all been done to them.'

The man's feelings of injustice and victimisation not only colour
his perception of himself and his relationship but sometimes are
transferred to the society which is seen as supporting women and
their actions. Many men feel they are unfairly treated by the court
system and in extreme cases their anger may be directed towards
judges who have made decisions about their divorce. The violence against Family Court judges is only one manifestation of
discontent and misdirected anger for divorcees unable to come
to terms with what has happened in their lives. Men often resent
decisions made about property and alimony, are frustrated at their
inability to prevent an unwanted divorce and are particularly bit-
ter about the most difficult of issue – care and responsibility for
their children.

In his research Jordan steered clear of the custody of children
issue because it has already received considerable attention. He
also feels it can be used to shift attention from the man's emotional reaction to his relationship breakup to the more socially
acceptable grief over the loss of children. Jordan did find that
almost all the men interviewed expressed very strong feelings
about being separated from their children – 98 per cent claimed
strong feelings for their children and 91 per cent did not want to
be separated from them.

Children or no children, it takes time to accept a marriage is
over and to establish a new life as a single person. As mentioned,
Jordan found that many men spend years clinging to false
hope – 55 per cent seek reconciliation, many make repeated
attempts to save their marriages. For many men the reality of sin-

gle life . . . lonely evenings, one-night-stands, dirty dishes . . . makes them all too aware of what they have lost. Jordan's research found men experience a range of problems in coping after separation, from difficulties at work, financial and domestic problems – house cleaning, washing, shopping, etc. and most of all, social isolation – difficulties in making new friends, developing and maintaining new relationships, finding people to talk to and feel close to.

For the man used to the devoted wife providing him with home comforts, it can be a dreadful shock to discover how much time and energy goes into keeping a house stocked with light bulbs and toilet paper, remembering to pick up the dry cleaning and getting time off work to meet the plumber to fix the leaky tap.

I have recently watched separated male friends rushing out to buy microwave ovens . . . and then use them solely for heating instant coffee and cold meat pies. You see them slinking around manchester departments appealing to motherly assistants for help in choosing curtain materials. Or, more often, taking the laundry home to mum or seeking out sleeping companions who not only provide sexual relief but, with a bit of luck, bacon and eggs.

Many single women are asked to provide a shoulder to cry on, to listen to stories of the wife who never understood him, who broke up his marriage and stole his children. Feeding the desolate man all your favourite whisky to drown his sorrows, sitting up in bed at three in the morning looking at photos of his children and hearing him sneak away before the dawn, unready yet to face the harsh light of a daytime relationship.

Men tend to turn to women – for sympathy; for someone to talk to. The irony is that in losing their wives they not only lose the person the feel closest to but also the one most able to help them cope with the loss. Divorce often makes men painfully aware of the lack of intimacy in their relationships with their male friends and their absolute dependence on their wives for emotional support.

A recently divorced friend told me of a business acquaintance whom he met soon after he separated. 'I'm sorry to hear about your divorce,' said the businessman, 'I know you won't want to talk about it.' Other men comment that their friends never mention the issue or recoil from the first sign of emotion.

Jordan found that more than a third of the men seek help from relatives and friends, many visit a marriage counsellor (20 per cent), general practitioner (18 per cent) or religious organisation (18 per cent), and 10 per cent seek psychiatric help.

Finding themselves in need, men are confronted by the stiff-upper lip tradition where real men never reveal the chinks in their armour.

As part of her research on friendship, American psychologist Lillian Rubin surveyed men to find out to whom they would turn if they were to come home one night and their wife announced she was leaving; 'One thirty-year-old Californian man who had just insisted that he had "20 intimate friends I can go to for just about anything" said he would call his mother in Michigan. I asked: "What about all those friends you've talked about, wouldn't you even go to one of them?" He replied quickly: "Sure, sure I would. But first I'd have to put myself together you know, get over the first shock, so I wouldn't just be falling apart".'

Yet they are falling apart, many of them – privately. They hide it from the world, bury themselves in their work, or fall into the lap or preferably the bed of the first available sympathetic woman, often remarrying long before they have begun to think about what really happened in the marriage and where it went wrong. Not that you ever really know – the complex interaction of two people's lives can never be neatly dissected to causes and conclusions. A short story by John Berryman sums it up; 'I gathered she "left" him – that is, kicked him out, as he more or less forced her to. In short, a usual case. Why people divorce each other is their own business, inscrutable. They seldom, in my experience, know why themselves – know what was most important, I mean, along the camps of the Everest of dissatisfactions nearly every human being feels with any other human being he knows inside out. Maybe nothing is more important. It's the mountain and you just get too weary to climb on.'

Weary or not, when faced with the harsh reality of being single, most men try desperately to cling to their mountain and when they slide off are all too ready to find new foothills to stumble through all over again.

The Man Shortage

From the single mother struggling to bring up the kids alone to the attractive mid-forties woman who has not had a date since her husband died four years ago to the glamorous divorcee who spends nights studying cabinet-making in the hope of meeting a mate, Australia has a female glut on the marriage market. The tide has turned in the 1980s.

Women outnumber men for the first time in the nation's history. For every 100 adult (over age fifteen) females, there are 97 males. This represents a surplus of 129,568 women. The field is wide open for the Aussie male seeking a mate, and the next twenty years promise a continuing oversupply of available women competing for the available men. The bad news for women on the hunt is that, if men seem thin on the ground now, the worst is yet to come.

The overall ratio of males to females does not mean very much in the mating game, a great deal of the oversupply being due to the swelling ranks of older women outliving their mates. Women over sixty-five, whom many would consider – unfairly perhaps – to be out of the race, account for most of the surplus. But this does not mean that everything is rosy in the ranks of younger women seeking suitable partners. They, too, are at a disadvantage – but it is of their own making. Women in Australia are creating a shortage of available partners through a tendency to choose men slightly older than themselves.

The supply and demand problem is due to the 'marriage gradient'. Women tend to marry 'up' – choosing partners above themselves in age, education, occupation and usually in height. Marrying older, more established males can enhance economic security. A counter-argument of course, is that males are choosing to marry down – needing the psychological security of a couple of extra years and extra status. Either way, it creates a big problem in countries with rising birth rates.

If women continue to partner slightly older men, each new group of women entering the marriage market finds itself competing for a slightly smaller group of males. This creates the 'marriage squeeze' which in the United States has produced severely restricted marital opportunities for all women past their mid-twenties.

The rapidly rising US birth rate in the 1950s meant that twenty years later, when these women entered the marriage market, they had to compete for smaller supplies of slightly older men. By 1970, for each 100 unmarried women aged twenty to twenty-four, only 84 unmarried men two years older were potential marriage partners. Among men three years older, there were only 67 potential husbands.

The US crisis has led to publication of a fascinating book, *Too Many Women* (Sage, New York 1983), in which social psychologists Marcia Guttentag and Paul F. Secord draw on cross-cultural and historical data to explore the impact on society of imbalance between the sexes. Their startling conclusion is that the imbalance may have contributed significantly to recent social trends in the US such as an increase in sexual freedom, including more pre-marital and extra-marital sex, delays in marrying and increased divorce and a stronger push by women for sexual, economic and political independence.

The marriage squeeze has hit Australia. Our 'baby boom' men

and women hit the marriage market in the late 1960s and early 1970s. Previously women had been advantaged in seeking partnerships by immigration policies which gave preference to the males required to build up Australia's labour force. The importation of hordes of males to construct the Snowy Mountains Scheme in the 1950s was one reason why the 'marriage squeeze' took longer to appear in Australia and was originally confined to smaller groups of women.

In 1971, women aged twenty-three to twenty-eight were the first group to taste the effects of the squeeze. For every 100 women aged twenty-three to twenty-five, there were 94 males two years older. (Like their American sisters, Australian women tend to choose men two years older. The median age of first marriage was 24.6 years for men and 22.4 for females in 1982.)

Most other women (up to sixty-five) still had plenty of choice, with sex ratios above 100 for each age group. (A 'sex ratio' refers to the number of available men per 100 women. A high sex ratio means more men than women.)

The scene for women had deteriorated further by 1976. More groups were experiencing low sex ratios. For every 100 women aged twenty-nine to thirty-one, there were now only 92 men. Almost all women up to forty and over fifty years of age were disadvantaged.

This brings us to today's picture and the prediction that the marriage squeeze will operate at least for the next twenty years, until the effect of the baby boom wears off, creating increasing problems – particularly for older women.

Brian English, family researcher at the University of New South Wales, is preparing a book on the Australian marriage market. Using population projections adjusted for probable trends in marriage, divorce and migration, he has calculated estimates of sex ratios in different age groups for the 1990s. He says; 'The marriage squeeze will continue well into the 1990s and have its greatest impact on women over thirty-five. Women who have not married by the age of thirty-five in 1990 and those divorced and widowed women seeking a second marriage will be in the "tightest" market situation this century. There will be only 65 available men for every 100 women. This represents a surplus of 58,000 women.'

Since the crux of the problem lies in the tendency for women to marry up (or men to marry down), the solution is obvious: The marriage squeeze would disappear if we could persuade women to marry younger men. English; 'At present, if all women were to marry men two years younger, the problem would be solved. By 1990, it will be necessary for women to marry men up to five years younger to eliminate the problem. Of course, the suggestion that women will increasingly be persuaded to marry younger men is treated with guffaws from men and women alike. But, if you examine the figures, the trend has already begun. Women are already finding the solution to their problem.' Indeed, if women aged twenty-five to twenty-nine were prepared to seek men five years younger, there would be three men for every woman (a sex ratio of 295!).

Women traditionally married up to find men who could provide them (and their children) with a roof over their heads and that usually meant a man rather older and more established in his career. With an oversupply of women, more women in their thirties and forties end up unattached at a time when many have established their economic independence and security. In these circumstances, a woman may be willing to forsake the bulging wallet for advantages offered by a younger – sprightly – mate. In 1983, a third of women aged forty to forty-four married men younger than themselves. Two-hundred and sixty-two women aged forty to forty-four married men ten years younger and 16 married men twenty years younger.

If we are to examine opportunities of men and women at different ages we also have to look at patterns of marriage, divorce and remarriage. We have to know who is out looking and who has retired from the hunt (retirement from the world of singles may prove temporary – one in four marriages ends in divorce).

Plenty of single people are keen to remain that way (but most will succumb to marriage at some stage) and many divorced, separated or widowed people vow 'never again'. We are concerned with the pool of potential partners for those who *are* interested and not just those seeking marriage partners but dating partners, companions, de facto spouses and lovers or simply someone to share the occasional night out at the bingo. In estimating the odds in the marriage market, we have to assume that *all* unmarried people *are* potentially available.

If we eliminate the married group from the pool of potentials, the picture looks even worse for women – particularly older women. The competition for available men has increased dramatically in recent years for women over thirty-five. For every 100 women aged thirty-five to thirty-nine on the hunt in 1981, there were only 69 potential partners.

Available women in their early sixties outnumbered their potential partners by almost four to one. By 1990, the situation will have improved for some but most women will have to look harder.

The chances of a woman finding a second partner after divorce become slimmer each year and worse the older she gets. This is roughly what is happening in the marriage market: Most people (86 per cent of men and 72 per cent of women) marry by the age of thirty – and a large proportion are into their second marriage by this stage. Of marriages of twenty-nine-year-olds in 1983, more than a third of the brides and almost a quarter of the bridegrooms were marrying for the second time. This has meant considerable movement in the marriage market, with partners chosen and discarded and new partners taking their places.

The vital question is; Who is left on the shelf? The answers are fascinating and have serious implications.

First, let's look at men and women who remain permanently single. Since the marriage gradient applies not only to age but also to education, income, occupation, etc, it would seem that the women left over are the achievers who cannot find anyone with whom to marry up. The never-married males would represent the bottom of the barrel – men whom no woman regards as better than herself.

The higher a woman's educational achievements, the more likely she is to remain single. Never-married women earn more than married women; they are also more likely to be in high status careers. Melbourne-based research by psychologist Yvonne Stolk shows that single women are twice as likely as married women to be in professional or managerial occupations. Single males generally have a lower socio-economic status than married or even divorced males – men with low levels of education and lower status jobs are more likely to be left out of the marriage market. Not that many people remain permanently unmarried. In 1981, there were 1,663,200 unmarried men over fifteen – but, once you sort out the men from the boys, the never-married thirties plus male is a rare bird indeed. Sixty-eight per cent of unmarried males are under twenty-five. Only 10 per cent of men and 5 per cent of women thirty-five years and over have never been married.

Since World War II, an increased proportion of people in Australia has married. But we are in the grip of low sex ratios. When this happens, more men and women remain single. Women remain single since they are unable to find suitable partners and men because of reduced pressure to marry. Male commitment is strongest when sex ratios are high and unattached women scarce. Women gain some power under these circumstances, based on their scarcity of numbers which offsets males' power associated with society's political, economic and legal structure.

Male commitment is weakest when sex ratios are low and men are scarce. They tend to delay marriage to keep their options open. The longer they do this, the more their power increases.

The male who remains single or divorces during his thirties or forties increases his market position through income job position, status, etc. He has his pick of partners from among the increasingly disadvantaged single women still in their twenties, younger divorced women also feeling the bite of low sex ratios and the divorced, never-married and widowed of his age and older. With this selection, the divorced man may bide his time before rushing back into marriage. Australian men have tended to remarry very quickly after divorce (average four years) and, since they marry younger women, they leave behind a pack of divorced women who have very few available men of their age or older.

The young woman who marries in her early twenties and divorces a few years later has a pretty good chance of remarrying. But, the longer she leaves it, the more her chances diminish. Her chances are further reduced if she has children – divorced single mothers are less likely to remarry than divorced childless women.

Ironically, women whose marriages have lasted longest are likely to be worst off if the marriage eventually deteriorates. The fifty-year-old woman whose husband scampers off in pursuit of his blonde secretary after twenty years of marriage will be competing with other middle-aged deserted or divorced wives and widows.

If a marriage is doomed, it is better for the woman to get out early while she still has a chance of finding a new partner. And that is happening. In Australia, divorces are happening earlier – the peak age group is the twenty-four to twenty-nine-year-olds and the evidence shows that women are making the decision to leave their husbands.

A national study of Australian women aged eighteen to thirty-nine conducted in 1984 by the market research company Product Development International for *Cleo* magazine found that women over thirty were having most of the difficulties finding suitable partners. Two-thirds of the single women in their thirties felt the available men 'were not worth the hassle of seeking out'. Almost a quarter associated their sex lives with a 'sense of loneliness and isolation' and a third claimed to be celibate by choice. More than a third said they met more interesting women than men.

Once again the marriage gradient must be part of the problem and, the more career and educational success the over-thirty woman achieves, the fewer available men keep up with her. Even so, these older single women show up in all the surveys (including the *Cleo* research) as predominantly self-assured and contented – often far more fulfilled than their married counterparts. They are also far from 'spinsterlike' in their sexual attitudes – the *Cleo* research found them to be sexually experimental and seek sexually adventurous partners, have high sexual expectations and be more likely than most women to accept the notion of a 'one-night stand'.

Alex Comfort, author of *The Joy of Sex*, once said the things that stop you from enjoying sex in old age are the same things that stop you from riding a bicycle – bad health, thinking it is silly and, no bicycle. The problem for many unattached women, even women in their thirties, is no bicycle (or at least none they regard worth riding).

But bicycle or no bicycle, the evidence is that many unattached women are relatively content with their lot. Melbourne research on never-married women by Robyn Penman and Yvonne Stolk (published in *Not the Marrying Kind*, Penguin, 1983) shows that, while a group of unattached women is anxiously seeking partners, many others accept being single and do not regard their status as failure.

There is also evidence that divorced women tend to adjust to being on their own – and are more likely to build fulfilling single lives than men are. The Matrimonial Property Enquiry found that, despite many women being financially disadvantaged by divorce, they have a remarkable degree of contentment.

Divorced males have more difficulty establishing a new life – partly because they have not usually precipitated the decision to separate. They are also less likely to have the support of friends.

The divorced woman most likely to suffer is the supporting mother. The growing numbers of single supporting mothers are leading to the increasing feminisation of poverty in this country. Single women with children are the fastest-growing group of welfare recipients – 76 per cent get pensions. This could be considered a consequence of low sex ratios.

The picture is further confused by homosexual men and women who are contributing to the swelling ranks of the never-married.

As it becomes more acceptable for homosexuals to live openly with same sex partners, it is likely the never married group will grow still further. At the moment there are also many homosexual men and women in the pool of divorced or separated people – previously many homosexuals married in an attempt to deny or 'cure' themselves of their homosexuality, or before they realised and accepted their sexual orientation. These previously married gays are unlikely to remarry, and hence contribute to the numbers of men and women who marry only once. In the future it seems unlikely that as many gays will follow the same course. (It does appear common for gay women to take time to discover their sexual preference and so many may continue to marry first). Experts believe there are many people who are bisexual by nature, being attracted to both males and females. With the increasing male shortage, it is possible that more bisexual women may choose lesbian partners and overt female homosexuality may be on the increase.

As for the common Sydney belief that there are few available men because they have all turned 'gay', homosexual men are simply a tantalising addition to the scene rather than a substitute for available heterosexual men. Homosexual men *and* homosexual women have flocked in recent years to Sydney from all over Australia and overseas. The men are more visible but homosexual spokesmen believe that just as many homosexual women are living in the area (estimates range from 100,000 to 200,000 of each sex).

What is happening has fascinating implications.

A young girl growing up in Australia and witnessing the effects of today's low sex ratio on the women before her will be pushed in various directions. She may choose to marry early and make every attempt to hang on to her man – a push toward a traditional conservative female role. In observing the plight of older unskilled women struggling to support families, she may postpone marriage to gain educational training for a career. With an increasing number of single, successful – apparently happy – women as her models, she may reject marriage. If she finds herself single in her thirties or forties and established in a career, she may marry or mate down. Incidentally, if she does so, she is more likely to find a partner willing to consider a more equal partnership – the evidence is that the younger the man, the more likely he is to accept a modern view of marriage as a partnership between equals.

According to Guttentag and Secord, low sex ratios tend to boost feminist movements. More women are likely to attain higher levels of education, making them more aware of career and lifestyle alternatives. Low sex ratios also mean more women are supporting themselves – and working women are generally more receptive to the feminist message.

Sexual liberation is also likely to gather steam during low sex ratio periods. As Guttentag and Secord show, whenever there is an abundance of women, men start to play around. They no longer need to commit themselves to one woman in exchange for sexual privileges. But this works against female sexual freedom in societies where women have an oversupply of men, because men use their social and political power to impose severe moral restraints on women, including social and legal sanctions on sexually liberated females.

The sexual revolution of the early 1970s, the increase in pre-marital and extra-marital sex and changes in sexual attitudes may have gained momentum through changes in sex ratios in Australia at that time. Evidence is available that women are having difficulty coping with the male flight from commitment and resent the loss of their sexual bargaining power.

It can be argued that sex was women's most valuable asset, their major source of power in a relationship – the promise of sex in exchange for the security of a man's commitment.

But the combination of today's more casual sexual attitudes and the female marriage market glut has meant that, as far as many men are concerned, the deal is off. A British newspaper once asked readers: 'What do men really want?' The answer from one female reader: 'Sex and chips'. Men know both are readily available. With or without marriage – they have their choice of dishes. The next two decades promise social scientists a great deal of entertainment in watching men cope with the smorgasbord.

Single Women

'I wonder why Janet has never married . . . she seems so nice.'

We've probably all said it, about some woman, sometime. What assumptions we all make about the lives of women who don't marry. She seems such a nice girl . . . what's wrong with her? Why hasn't she done it? Hasn't she ever been asked?

It probably says more about ourselves, our hopes, our delusions than it does about the lives of unmarried women. What does marriage mean to us that makes it so easy for us to judge the people who choose another path? That's the first assumption, you see. People who *choose* another path. Some women, many women are unmarried by choice . . . chance plays a part but there are women who stride through life with such confidence that they don't need marriage in the same way the rest of us do. Women who have always been filled with a sense of their own destiny, women who have never needed a man to make them whole.

Julia is now eighty. She has studied, travelled, worked, accomplished and is well-known in Sydney for her achievements in the social welfare field. She knew all along that marriage was not a priority. She remembers being puzzled by her schoolfriends determinedly filling glory boxes: 'I was never very enamoured of the idea of marriage,' she says.

It is strange talking to her. A woman who grew up at a time when there were even greater pressures on women to marry than there are now. Yet she exhibits such an easy acceptance of the fact that she was a creature apart, a university-educated woman at a time when few women were so, a strong and independent person quite different from the women most men of that time expected to marry. Most men? Well, the pickings were even leaner then . . . the men of her generation were the veterans of the First World War – or what was left of them.

Talking to her makes a mockery of many of our assumptions about unmarried women. Of course she was asked: 'There were plenty of opportunities to marry; lots of offers. They were nice people, nice men but I was a strong woman and I didn't want to end up mothering a man. I saw other girls being married, giving up all that freedom. Being in love, marrying means you don't care if you mother a man – I couldn't do that. I always thought I was captain of my own soul.'

She knew it all along – master of my fate, captain of my soul. For Julia it came as a surprise to discover that some people pitied her. 'It had never occured to me. Someone said to me a few years ago: "Oh, how terrible, you've never married . . ."' It obviously amused her, this strange perception of her life: 'I think I've had a damned good innings.'

For other women, less secure women, the knowledge that they don't need marriage to live happily ever after comes much later in their lives. For Lynn it marked the end of a desperate period in her thirties when she had a vision of herself becoming a middle-aged spinster – 'ugly, dried up and alone, marked forever as a freak and a failure'. She made a last-ditch effort to end her aloneness. She moved from the country town where she lived, re-established her career, joined organisations where she could meet people. She met men, sometimes had affairs that lasted for years. Then finally after a long and painful process her self-esteem reappeared. 'I came to realise there wasn't anyone who could assume a basic part of me, nor could I or would I want to surrender any part of myself. There is no one who can complete me – make me whole – no more than I can complete someone else. *There are no others.* I felt that I was therefore all I had but my sense of selfhood was whole, precious and very sweet.'

For women who achieve that 'sweet sense of selfhood', who accept and enjoy their single status, the rest of their lives often seems relatively smooth sailing. Some, like Lynn, will look back on their 'single panic' fever with regret: 'My biggest regret is that I put so much of my life energy into coping with being single. For three years I was just drained.'

Women in their forties and fifties who enjoy being single impress with their confidence, their self-esteem, particularly when contrasted with the turmoil many married women face – children leaving home, husbands in career crises, trying to find work after years of playing mother.

Therein lies one of the great ironies in the situation of unmarried women. Universally they are pitied, treated as unnatural. There is a jarring contrast between the self-perceptions and self-esteem of these women and the attitude of society towards them.

For her book *Our Lives for Ourselves – Women Who Have Never Married* (G P Putman & Sons, New York, 1981), author Nancy L. Peterson asked the women she interviewed to rank categories of women in terms of their perceived status in society . . .

The unmarried women believed married women had the highest status, followed by widows: 'a married woman has more status because it means somebody wanted her, somebody chose her'; 'it means she was picked'; 'women are supposed to get married and get rewarded for it'.

Widows rated highly because their singleness was sad and involuntary: 'a widow has done the expected thing and the fact she is single is not of her own choosing'.

The never-married women were not sure who ranked next: either themselves or divorced women. There was a tendency to imagine that divorced women out-ranked never-married women, because divorced women once had married – done the right thing

– despite the fact that they had failed. Unmarried women generally saw their own status as bottom of the barrel, the lowest of all.

Can you imagine what that feels like – to be satisfied with your life but to live in a society which pities you – to know that people constantly wonder why, wonder if you have ever been asked? The social pressures are immense and the hurt these women feel is illustrated by the eagerness with which women of all ages – eighty, sixty, fifty, thirty – hastened to tell me they *had* received offers. They needed to prove that if they were on the shelf, it was by choice. Even talking to a group of women in their early twenties within ten minutes I had heard of each proposal, each possibility.

Yet even the women living day-in, day-out with these pressures acknowledged that they too judge other unmarried women by the same criteria. They tar them with the very brush that has caused them so much hurt. Thea is forty-one, an attractive, vivacious businesswoman running her own PR firm. She is quite happy to admit she makes judgments about other unmarried women. 'If I meet a woman of thirty-five to fifty I know there is a question mark in my mind. Why isn't she married? And I do leap to conclusions. If she's dreary you think, oh well, that explains it, she's a bit of a bore, who'd want to talk to her? Oh yes, no one would have asked her.' Thea was asked – the first time in her twenties – but she knew there was so much she wanted to do first. She was in a rush to get on with it.

You get the impression Thea has got on with it all, she's travelled, done well, leads a busy life full of people – the gay social whirl. Along the way she's acquired a realistic view of marriage and what it would mean to someone like her. 'After all the racing around, sometimes I like the idea of a one-to-one relationship, the home comforts, all that bit. I know marriage is a lot of work. Most women are happy to do it and I'm sure I would feel the same. You live for your man and with that comes all that devotion, dedication, hard work. It's a very unselfish existence and I think in the majority of cases women enjoy it. But I've come to terms with the likelihood I won't get married. I enjoy being single. It's a selfish life but a great one.'

It's funny that. The women who enjoy being single feel guilty about it. They all mentioned feeling selfish, guilty about their freedom, the choices in their lives. When they compare themselves to married women they feel vaguely guilty that they don't envy the women who have done the right thing, chosen the path expected of them.

As more women end up remaining single – a likely event in view of the unbalanced sex ratios currently operating in this country – perhaps this guilt will disappear. The problem for many women up till now is they have had very few successful role models, very few successful happy advertisements for the single life to show them the way. This contrasts with the situation for men. There seem always to have been prominent, apparently happy bachelors flaunting themselves and their lifestyles, offering an alternative to the married life. It was a concept sufficiently powerful to launch a magazine, *Playboy*, a magazine which is claimed to have contributed significantly to the increasing male flight from commitment to marriage and family responsibility.

But part of the problem for the contented single woman is the resentment she sometimes encounters from married women bogged down in the hard work of marriage – the constant care and attention, compromising, nurturing. Laura, another attractive, unmarried career woman in her early forties, tells of the hurt she experienced when attacked by her sister-in-law for the fulfilment she gains from her career. 'She told me that I could achieve so much only because I didn't have a man in my life. If I had a man I wouldn't be able to do all these things. If I had a man who really loved me it just wouldn't be possible.'

Laura does have men in her life, as do most unmarried women. She is presently living with a man, and has had numerous relationships in the past. She, too, started off looking longingly through the windows of bridal shops, dreaming of rings and things. But then she moved away from her small home town, away from her friends stampeding to the altar and travelled overseas. There, for the first time: 'I didn't feel like a leper in my society. I had escaped from the people back home who kept wondering what was wrong, why I hadn't done it. I had plenty of relationships but it was never quite right.' Laura still believes in a marriage, still sees it as a possibility for herself, but having witnessed the breakdown of her parents' marriage, she is cautious and basically content.

For women who resist the early pressures, who avoid that first rush to the altar, caution often seems to set in. They watch the marriages of their friends, witness the hurt, help divorced friends pick up the pieces of their lives. The view they gain of marriage is far from the happily-ever afters of the romance stories; 'I've seen so many bad marriages and divorces and I listen to the things people say about why their marriage broke up and I know I'm not infallible, I'm just another person, so what would make my marriage so different from all the ones I hear about? And it's just scary, I don't know. And then people say, "Well, it's a risk, everything in life is a risk", but I think it's a big risk because you're playing with your life and somebody else's life and you can do irreparable damage to yourself and to another person, or to your children.'

When you talk to women, married and unmarried, about what's involved in marriage there are phrases which keep coming up; 'It's a commitment, a statement that you'll do your best to stay together'; 'it must involve compromises, you have to accommodate to another person'; 'it's proof of our ability to make relationships work'; 'when you're just living together if the going gets tough you can just piss off – it's too easy'; 'it's hard work but it's worth all the effort.'

Hard work, compromise, unselfish – it makes it sound like doing penance, doesn't it? Trial by marriage, can you survive the test? It's a funny notion and makes you wonder why it's still so attractive, why we rush like lemmings towards this fate . . .

This hit home to me talking to Jane, a very bright nineteen-year-old with anything but a romantic view of marriage; 'All my friends want desperately to get married and assume it will last forever, or else they say you have to work very hard at it. I think that's dreadful,' she said. 'I've seen so many women who do work very hard at their marriages but often the man seems to do very little. The women seem to compromise themselves so much more than the men.' Jane realises it's not all bad. 'Obviously there are gains, joys in being together, bringing up children, but there are also a lot of disadvantages too. And it's not a fair deal.'

We all know how true that is. All the research shows that men look forward to being married. Married men are one of the most contented groups in our society, secure, sane, emotionally stable. Single men, on the other hand, don't do nearly as well in the happiness stakes – and married women come off worst of all. For the past thirty years research has poured out showing that married women often end up neurotic, under stress, suffering from depression, lack of self-esteem.

There's nothing like a cynical nineteen-year-old to cut through the romantic haze; 'I think many people marry for security, because they are afraid of being alone, because they conform to social pressures. They marry for status. But it's crazy.'

Must marriage be a sacrifice to the altar of compromise? Surely it doesn't have to be so unequal? Some women do manage to negotiate the contract and have a more equal relationship.

Jane; 'I just can't believe in marriage as it is. I don't think it is feasible. How can one person satisfy all parts of another person, fulfil all my needs? It's hard to find one person you enjoy sexually, enjoy mentally, who wants to share everything you do. Yet so many married couples get jealous if their partners spend lots of time with other people. They smother each other. And besides, people change. They grow in different directions, but then it's too late. You're bound together and divorce hurts. Maybe you can renegotiate the marriage contract but there are all those dreadful feelings of possessiveness and jealousy and rules to get away from first. I just don't understand how people can bound into it with such enthusiasm.'

Well, not all do, and many of the women who end up not marrying remain single because they have been wary of the very issues Jane feels so strongly about. Yvonne Allen is a psychologist running a marriage agency in Sydney which has established a reputation for a professional, sensitive approach quite different from many of its sleazy competitors. Her agency attracts a large number of women, often professionals, highly qualified career women who have remained single because of their unwillingness to accept a traditional view of marriage where women do so much of the compromising.

Yvonne says; 'They are very confident women, sure of what they want and they aren't prepared to give it all up. They want a relationship but not just on his terms.'

I spoke to some of them and patterns emerged similar to those among women I had spoken to previously: past relationships not working out; energy spent on careers; travelling and moving away from roots, from tradition; a question of timing and circumstances rather than a matter of deliberate choice.

'All in all, I think a lot of women like me are not married out of pure accident or because "the numbers" won't support us. Many of us are late bloomers, and lost out because our faster developing sisters got there first. And often we look for a situation on our own terms – and a lot of men are not up for negotiation.'

These women had obviously not turned their backs on marriage entirely and many in fact approached Yvonne Allen's agency as a last ditch attempt to find a partner. Lynn, a tall and glamorous career woman, is now forty-five. She watched other unmarried friends come to terms with being single, happy in their careers, travelling every year or two – gradually giving up relationships with males and living their lives for themselves. This was not for her. 'It worried me. I felt I had to do something – it wasn't good enough to keep waiting for something to happen. I didn't want to live the rest of my life as a single person and this year decided to make an effort to push fate!'

So here she is, undergoing the painful process of following up agency introductions, stewing when men don't call back after the first date, forcing herself to make the phone calls she never used to make.

'Fish or cut bait.' It's an expression used by a woman to describe her decision whether to hunt for a man or accept being single, perhaps forever. Lynn is fishing. So is Patricia, a school teacher aged forty-eight. Her story is even more poignant. Of all the women I spoke to, she was the hardest. No talk of a sense of self-hood here, just a sense of loss, of having missed out. She speaks of a few previous relationships, of having loved someone who was not free, of her feelings not reciprocated. But the real energy of her life was devoted to the care of her mother, who died last year after six years in a nursing home. Six years spent travelling for hours to spend time with her uncomplaining mother, forced to close her eyes to the hideous circumstances in which her mother spent her last years, crying sometimes in her car, returning home to no one.

Yet the worst came recently when her mother finally died. Coping not with grief – she had lived with that for years – but with the dreadful, frightening knowledge that she was no longer needed. The barbs, the cruelties which bounce off other, more confident, unmarried women strike home here. Dorothy tells of the time she walked in on a conversation between two married female friends and they abruptly stopped talking. She learned later they were discussing what to do when children interrupt parents' sex play. You could *feel* the hurt, the assumption that sexuality was not part of this woman's life, the exclusion. I remembered a paraplegic telling me a similar story: his mates stopped telling sexy jokes whenever he was around. To them he had become a sexless freak.

And through Patricia's eyes, you see the other side of marriage. The companionship that would end her loneliness, the pleasure of caring for a man, of knowing you are needed. And you hope for her – against all odds – that she will find a man to match her sensitivity, her intelligence, her need.

It's too late for her to know the other blessing of marriage – the part which for many makes it all the more worthwhile. I haven't even spoken about the issue of children, the biological urges which make the thirties such a stressful time for many single women. So many articles have been written on the pressures on women who feel the time for motherhood fast running out. Just one point here: new medical technology and a more realistic knowledge of risks of late motherhood seem to be pushing the deadline for marriage and motherhood further towards forty. When I was growing up thirty was the age of decision, the point at which you were left on the shelf. Young women I spoke to for this article now see that crisis period nearer thirty-five to forty.

But whatever the exact age, the biological clock still exerts real pressure on every new relationship involving a woman in her thirties. Men have often talked to me of the discomfort they feel when they date a mid-thirties woman, their awareness that they are being sized up as a prospective sperm donor and future father. Often the man in this age group is divorced and has already had children – the 2 am feed no longer holds much attraction. Alternatively, he may have avoided the responsibilities of marriage and children only through strenuous evasive action – to see the new love of his life clucking over passing baby carriages is enough to set the red lights flashing. Even the men who are willing or even keen to have children may experience some discomfort at the pressure they feel to get on with the job. By the late thirties there's little time for honeymoon periods or tasting the joy of childless coupledom. There's no doubt that coming to terms with a childless future is *the* most difficult issue many single women have to face.

'I think I would have been a good mother,' Patricia said wistfully. She tells of the three-year-old child who rings and says: 'I want to come and sleep with you,' and laughs; 'I don't get many offers like that.'

Different women, different lives. Through their eyes so many different views of marriage, that most perplexing institution. And to end it all a happy ever after story in true *Women's Weekly* tradition.

Pamela, now aged thirty-two, until last year had never been kissed, or touched or desired. She had grown up uninterested, indifferent to the boy/girl romances of her school friends – she rejected the dates which came her way. Men were just friends, colleagues as she concentrated on work and her career. It was not just indifference – there must have been a touch of fear, a legacy of lessons well learned from her mother about sex being dirty, something men wanted, women feared. She lived at home with parents who with almost unseemly haste bestowed on her a spinster status by her mid-twenties. She should accept her lot and be content, they told her. She could stay with them and look after them.

Then two years ago her body took control. Her life changed. She had an operation to remove cysts which were destroying her reproductive organs. The hero of this story is the doctor, a gynae-cologist who, sensing the naivety and ignorance of his chaste patient, sat down with her and talked. About sexuality, about her body and the pleasure it could give her, about the fact that time was running out to seize the slim chance that now remained to have children. He gave her books to read and she read, learned about herself and discovered she had sexual feelings and desires she had never before experienced. She read about men and their feelings and started wondering – and finally dared to hope.

Last year she too went to Yvonne Allen and for the first time went out with men, nervous, conscious of her strangeness, her maidenhood. And yes, she did meet her man. Despite the pro-tests of her mother, reluctant to let go of her Peter Pan daughter and household slave, this week they are to be married. It sent shivers up my spine talking to her. Her dream has come true . . . she can't believe it. Hearing all this, for a moment I couldn't help but push all doubts aside and join her in that fairyland world where marriage is a woman's crowning achievement.

It's a cop out, isn't it? A sell out of all the women who enjoy living their lives for themselves, who reject the pressures towards social conformity. The rest of us marry or long for marriage and, if we're very lucky, tilt at a few windmills along the way.

The Mateship Myth

Mateship – it's part of the Australian heritage. The male heritage, born in the bush in colonial days, nurtured in the male-dominated isolation of cattle stations and gold fields, glorified by the Anzacs . . . every man had his mate, his partner, standing silently by his side.

Silence was the essence of traditional mateship – that friendship based on unspoken bonds, shared unvoiced emotions. The scene has been played over and over again. The gaunt man stands at his wife's funeral. His mate comes up, says nothing, but rests a gentle hand briefly on his shoulder. The farmer lays down his rifle after slaughtering the last of his cattle. His offsider grunts in sympathy and turns tactfully away. The man greets his long-lost friend at the airport, hands stretched out, his face alight with pleasure . . . and a moment later pulls away from the embrace and cracks a joke to cover his embarrassment.

At these times of high emotion, nothing is said. Perhaps, as many men would argue, nothing *needs* to be said.

At other times, men, mates *do* talk, . . . holding up the bar, nursing their tinnies side by side at the footy, wandering around the golf course, tinkering with a car, pondering over a chess game.

Men talk, but rarely about anything personal. Recent research on friendship, both here and overseas, has shown that male relationships are based on *shared activities*: men tend to *do* things together rather than simply *be* together. When male friends meet, it is for a purpose; like sharing a beer, or having a game of squash, or trying out a new machine and their conversation is often focussed around these activities. In between comparing notes on fishing techniques or new computer software they talk of other things. Of current events, work, business, sports, politics . . . the focus is on external events, things which happen 'out there'. Rarely do men exchange private or personal information, rarely is there much self-disclosure.

That's what makes male friendships so different from relationships between women. Female friendships, particularly close friendships, are usually based on self-disclosure, or on talking about intimate aspects of their lives.

It's the talk which makes the difference. Surely you've noticed it. Just think about that modern instrument of communication, the telephone. You must have heard men complain about the amount of time women spend talking on the telephone to their friends, 'I just can't understand what they find to talk about . . . natter, natter, natter.' In the busy life of the modern women, particularly the working woman, the telephone is the only means she has of maintaining the verbal intimacy which is essential to her friendships. Men telephone other men for information, to make arrangements, for brief exchanges rather than baring of souls. They arrange to meet certain friends for certain things – golf-playing friends, squash friends, friends from work and with each of these friends will share a part of their lives, a part of themselves, but rarely is a friend allowed close enough to know all.

Professor Robert Bell is a sociologist now at Temple University in Philadelphia, USA. In the mid-1970s, he studied friendship patterns in Australia as part of a five year research project completed in the USA. Bell found that, despite all the Australian hype about mateship, Australian men differed little from their American counterparts, with relatively few males claiming close friendships with other men and most men maintaining their guard, even in their most intimate relationships with each other.

Here, and later in the USA, Bell had some difficulty finding males willing to discuss friendship. Not infrequently he encountered men who claimed to have no male friends. His final results showed men claim an average of 3.2 close friends compared to 4.7 for the women he studied. Ten percent of the males in his research claimed no close friends – this was virtually unknown amongst the women.

Previous research on friendship has shown men will often claim more acquaintances than women. Since men frequently meet in groups for shared activities they collect more 'friends of the road' than women do. But when it comes to 'friends of the heart', exclusive one-to-one friendships, males fall behind. American psychologist Lillian Rubin has just published a book on friendship based on interviews with over 300 men and women – *Just Friends – The Role of Friendship in Our Lives* (Harper & Row, New York, 1985). Rubin comments on the fact that past research has often reported males as having more friends than females, 'but this has to do with men's propensity for naming as a friend anyone with whom they have some ongoing association – co-workers, neighbours, tennis partners, members of the bowling team, while women tend to use the term "friend" more selectively.'

Her study painted a different picture; 'The results of my own research are unequivocal. At every life stage between twenty-five and fifty-five, women have more friendship, as distinct from collegial relationships or work mates, than men, and the differences in the content and quality of their friendships are marked and unmistakeable.'

The differences Rubin refers to are, in part, due to the fact that male friendships tend to be locked into shared experiences, and when the experience ends, often the friendship goes with it. So when the damaged knee flares up and squash is no longer on the agenda, the squash friendship goes by the board. This applies even to the close bonding which results from shared danger or isolation. Ex-war buddies, old Anzacs, may certainly meet and relive past experiences, remember shared emotions, but rarely do these experiences lead to continuing closeness when back in the real world.

With women, intense emotions tend to have the opposite effect on the development of friendships. A shared experience, particularly one involving extreme emotion, is very likely to lead to the formation of a deeper bond and lasting friendship. There are endless stories of women who meet as patients in a hospital ward, infertility clinic, as parents of children with drug problems, or survivors of a flood or a fire, and form secure relationships. At these times female intimacy is easily achieved and naturally maintained.

Males caught with their emotional pants down may initially take some comfort from the presence of another male but eventually are left feeling exposed and uncomfortable. Displays of emotion and self-revelation often create barriers to developing male relationships rather than paving the way for further disclosure.

Norm Radican, senior researcher at Macquarie University's Department of Sociology, is involved in a research project on the experience of masculinity – 'interviewing men about being men'. Originally from the United States, Radican has been involved in numerous workshop and education courses on men, relationships and sexuality. He tells stories of males who, in times of crisis, such as a marriage break-up, or personal tragedy such as the death of a child, do reach out to other men, and find later that the self-disclosure has created tension in the friendship, it has erected barriers rather than removed them. 'They know they have broken the rules, the carefully prescribed codes of behaviour which underlie male friendships. Men know there are things you can and can't talk about. You don't talk honestly about how you are feeling; you don't admit to being depressed or sad. It's okay to make a joke of it, but not to reveal yourself. That's not acting like a man.'

Just as humour can be used to reveal feelings, it is also used as a defence against intimacy. So, on those rare occasions when a man does mention something that's worrying him, some cause of unhappiness, . . . often one of his mates will release the tension, pass it off with a joke. Pulling him back into line, stopping him from revealing too much, or going too far. Humour is used as a form of censure, a casual put-down of volunteered feelings that saves the volunteer from embarrassment by acknowledging that surely he was joking. It's also used as a means of affection – 'you old son of a bitch' – the crude nicknames, the endearing insults that are part and parcel of everyday pub talk. It's all part of a carefully constructed system which constrains male friendships to safe, acceptable limits; 'If I really showed my feelings, the other guys would eat me alive. It's too dog-eat-dog out there to be honest about the things that really count to you . . . You can't leave yourself wide open like that.'

Dog eat dog. Are males really afraid of being honest with each other for fear of retribution? From his group work with men, Radican believes male friendships are inhibited by the competitiveness bred into males. 'Men are taught as little boys at school to compete with each other; to win games, to win girls, and then later to win jobs, promotion, success. Life for many men is a competition. You learn to play your cards close to your chest and not to give away things that could be used against you.'

Radican is running a sensuality group for males, a course which teaches men it is possible to be honest with other men about sex. 'Sexuality is a topic most males are extremely nervous of discussing honestly with other males – it's a classic area where men compete. They lie to each other about thier exploits. They never reveal their fears about performance or share their failures. The men in my groups are always amazed to find they can talk honestly about such things – but they'll only talk because they are strangers to each other. If their friends were there, they'd be forced to cover up. They wouldn't want their friends to have that sort of knowledge about them.'

For males, knowledge is power. By withholding parts of themselves from others, they feel they are protecting themselves. They feel less vulnerable. Robert Bell's research showed over two-thirds of the males he studied acknowledged there were topics they wouldn't discuss with their male friends. Bell records the comments of a thirty-eight-year-old executive: 'I have three close friends I have known since we were boys and they live here in the city. There are some things I wouldn't tell them. For example, I wouldn't tell them much about my work because we have always been highly competitive. I certainly wouldn't tell them about my feelings of any uncertainties with life or various things I do. And I wouldn't talk about any problems I have with my wife or in fact anything about my marriage and sex life. But other than that I would tell them anything. [After a brief pause he laughed and said:] That doesn't leave a hell of a lot, does it?' (*Worlds of Friendship*, Robert R. Bell., Sage Publications, London, 1981.)

Another recent study on male relationships, *The McGill Report on Male Intimacy* (Michael E. McGill, Holt, Rinehart and Winston, New York, 1985) found one in ten males has a friend with whom he discusses work, money, marriage; only one in twenty has a friendship where he discusses his feelings about himself or his sexual feelings.

Competition between males isn't the only barrier to male intimacy. There is another even more potent force – homophobia.

Homophobia. It's the fear of being seen as homosexual, fear of being called a queer, of having one's masculinity questioned. 'What are you, a fag?' Homophobia is rampant, an unspoken, often barely conscious fear which prevents males from being close to each other, touching one another, from showing affection, even from being alone with other men. How many men would feel comfortable asking another male over for dinner, for a drink? How many men would accompany other males to the movies, alone?

It's often assumed that the fear is of what lies within, the latent homosexual who denies his inner nature by denouncing what he fears he will become. It's an unlikely explanation based on Freudian assumptions which are now being questioned. Modern thinking suggests homophobia has nothing to do with fear of latent homosexuality but rather is based on a fear of women, of behaving in an unmasculine, feminine manner. Lillian Rubin believes the problem stems from the fact that the male's first identification is with his mother – it is a female who gives him his first sense of self. Then, in order to establish his gender identity, to identify his maleness, the male has to relinquish his identification with his mother, to renounce the female aspects of his nature. So, Rubin argues, being a male involves a constant struggle to reject the female aspects of oneself – a struggle which men can only win by denying their own emotions and carefully monitoring their own behaviour.

So the edifice of masculinity rests on uncertain foundations. To be male requires constant public proof of *not* being female. The real threat is of being seen as sissy. What confuses the issue is the fact that homosexuality has come to be associated with effeminate behaviour. Homosexuals are wrongly assumed to behave in a feminine manner; to be more emotional, to enjoy traditional female activities, not to behave like men. And even though most males now realise that homosexuals don't necessarily wear pink shirts, burst into tears, carry flowers, or go to the ballet any more than heterosexuals do, to indulge in such behaviour still carries some association with homosexuality. As recent research shows, the men who are most nervous of being labelled gay are *not* latent homosexuals, but rather traditional, conservative males who cling to rigid sex roles as public proof of their own masculine identity. They are men who are afraid of change in their lives and in their relationships.

And so the men who embrace on the football fields or cling to each other in bars aren't revealing hidden sexual desires, but rather a normal human need for closeness and physical contact. Unfortunately for men, in our society it is only the supermasculine who are permitted such public displays of affection – the athletes, the footballers whose masculinity is unquestionable, and the drunk or pretended drunk who uses the cover of alcohol to allow behaviour which otherwise would not be permitted.

The rest of the time, the barriers are up. Men keep each other at bay maintaining comfortable, undemanding, fair-weather friendship; 'I know several guys that I would feel perfectly comfortable talking to about whatever I wanted to. Just because we don't spend all of our time revealing our innermost personal feelings to each other doesn't mean that we couldn't or wouldn't talk about those things if the occasion demanded it.'

We could be close . . . if the occasion demanded it. This quote from McGill's book comes to the crunch. What happens in these fair-weather friendships when a man *does* need someone to talk to. The evidence from counsellors, doctors, etc, from people who end up picking up the pieces when a man is in emotional trouble, is that often men can't bring themselves to talk to friends when they need them most. In Sydney, there's an organisation known as Dial-a-Mum, a voluntary group of women, of mothers who offer telephone counselling to people in need. Dial-a-Mum gets its fair share of calls from men, men in trouble who often have no one else to talk to. Wendy Finlayson, founder of Dial-a-Mum finds often the men comment that they have no close friends, their only real friend is their wife. This means, of course, that when the problem lies with the wife, or the marital relationship, they are out on their own. So Dial-a-Mum is there to help the men cope . . . when the wife walks out, or is having an affair, or announces she is lesbian or is angry, upset, or communication simply grinds to a halt.

Often by the time a man wishes to reach out to other men, the emotional restraint which typifies male friendships has reached the point of paralysis. After all, it starts very early. Psychologists Wyndol Furman and Howard Markman at the University of Denver in Colorado, conducted experiments with pairs of unacquainted eight to nine-year-old girls and boys. The pairs of girls and boys were placed in a room together, given a pile of Lego and their talk recorded by a hidden camera.

The boys tended to play with the Lego and limited their conversation mainly to the technicalities of Lego making. The girls, well, they fiddled a bit with the Lego but most of their talk and their energy was devoted to the business of getting to know each

other. They asked questions, disclosed personal information
– where they lived, what school they went to, what it was like
having to wear braces, etc. etc. At the end of the period the girls
had shared three times more information about themselves than
the boys.

When it's a girl-boy pair, it's the female who prods and pokes
at the male, forcing him to reveal himself . . . and he usually does.
With a female, he's not threatened by competition or homophobia. Apart from his wife, often a man's best friend *will* be another
woman. McGill's research showed two-thirds of the men he interviewed had disclosed personal information to at least one woman
other than their spouses, a third reported they revealed things
about themselves to another woman they had not revealed to their
wives. There's the female workmate to whom he confesses his
ambitions and his fears about his career, the sister who knows
all about his finances, the old girlfriend to whom he talks about
his marriage. It's often a tricky relationship with the possibility
of developing into a sexual affair, clouding and confusing what
is otherwise a rare opportunity for intimacy.

Naturally, such relationships can be difficult to maintain, and
hard for a wife to understand. If you are a woman who has been
desperately trying to get your husband to communicate, it is mad-
dening to know there are others in your husband's life with access
to information he never reveals to you.

For even though it is usually the wife who knows more about
her husband than anyone else, the male's emotional constipation
often prevents him from revealing all even in this most intimate
of all his relationships. McGill tells stories of husbands who hide
from their wives financial worries, crises at work, health
problems, all sorts of personal anxieties and fears. Working as
a sex therapist, I often saw men who had never been able to discuss a sexual problem with their wives. Men who watched endless
late late shows on television rather than risk going to bed and
facing their impotence. Women who were unable to get their husbands to admit anything was wrong – or even to discuss it. A
Sydney-based service providing mid-career advice for displaced

executives found a number of men who had maintained a facade of employment for months after being retrenched leaving each day for work, briefcase in hand, only to spend the day hidden away in an unknown pub before returning on schedule.

But even if a wife is a man's best friend, his sole confidant, that too can create problems. Dependent as they are on the exclusive intimacy of their marital relationship, men often resent the fact that women go outside the relationship, revealing details of family life to their friends; using friends for support, for comfort, for marital advice. Men know women talk to other women about all aspects of their marriage, even their sexual problems – and for the man that often feels like a betrayal.

As men grow older, their circle of friends tends to shrink and they become more dependent on their wives for companionship and support. Whereas women continue to make friendships throughout their lives, men as they become less mobile often have less opportunity for their activity-bound friendships. The retired man loses touch with work friends, his health interferes with shared sporting activities. And then if his best friend, his wife, dies, he's left alone, facing increasing isolation. Whereas the widow usually has friends and close relatives to help her through her bereavement, the elderly widower is less likely to be part of a social network.

The loss of his sole means of emotional support often has tragic consequences – as evidenced by the early mortality and high suicide rate of bereaved males as compared to females. Yes, he often has another option – a new woman. As someone said, men replace, women mourn. It's sometimes the only way he copes.

There's a classic story about male friendship. Tom meets his old mate Harry on the street corner;

'How's it going, Harry?'

'Fine, Tom, fine.'

'Business?'

'Never better.'

'And the operation?'

'Piece of cake.'

A few weeks later Tom is astonished to discover that when Henry died from post-operative complications he was technically insolvent.

A joke. Unfortunately, it's all too common for males to discover long after the event that a friend, a mate, has suffered in silence through a personal crisis. The irony is that often men hide from each other experiences and emotions they all share – the facade of the infallible, invulnerable man is maintained by their silence. Recently the women's movement has highlighted the strength of female friendships – close relationships which for many women heighten the highs and soften the lows in their lives. Many men are still left floundering, isolated from each other by myths of mateship which serve only to maintain barriers to male intimacy and mutual comfort. But luckily, it's changing as more and more males learn to discard the hollow bonds of mateship for genuine, close friendships with other men.

Confessions of a Superwoman

You see them everywhere. Schlepping home from work with a briefcase over one arm and shopping bags in the other. Waiting impatiently in the lunch hour for the child to emerge from the dentist in time to drop him back to school and get back to work. Picking up the take-away chicken, hoping to disguise it sufficiently that the guests won't notice.

These are the superwomen, the new breed of working women who are struggling to combine their roles as mothers and wives with the demands of their careers. It's true, it's certainly not easy. Their lives are inflated like tyres to the maximum pressure. The responsibilities are immense, the rewards often lost through sheer exhaustion.

But there's another side to the superwoman story, the good side. The truth is that despite the hard work and juggling required to keep the different facets of the frantic life afloat, the 'superwoman' has one marvellous compensation. Being busy and being seen to be busy lets you off the hook. Buys you a way out of all aspects of your many roles you secretly despise . . . like cleaning cupboards, or attending P & C meetings, or weekend training seminars, or entertaining your husband's business friends. When you combine wife, mother, career and all, each role becomes the perfect excuse for avoiding the worse aspects of the other.

I've always known that. The busier I become, the more comfortable I am about cutting corners and making things do. That's the great advantage of life as a 'superwoman' – the more hats you wear, the less fussy you are about any of them.

Good enough, considering. It's the secret motto of the superwoman. You may never write that novel but having a few articles published here and there is pretty good considering you have two children to look after. You don't give many dinner parties but the odd brunch isn't bad considering you work full time. You end up buying the cake to wrap in greaseproof for selling at the school fete but you know the children don't really mind, considering . . . (we hope).

The more eggs you have in your basket the less you need to torment yourself if one doesn't hatch out quite as planned. With just one egg, just one role, there's such a dreadful obligation to be awfully good at it. Looking after the house for instance. If you are there all the time you can't help but notice those hairy black things growing in the vegetable drawer and that ominous smell behind the children's cupboard. The dripping tap must eventually get on your nerves, and there's *no* excuse for running out of toilet paper.

All you need is a good time-consuming job, a few evening meetings, an extra obligation or two and suddenly priorities change. The dripping tap becomes much more bearable permanently stuffed with a flannel, and when you are only home at night the kitchen floor looks quite clean – particularly when a few light bulbs blow and aren't replaced. Then joy of joys, all of a sudden you're regarded as too busy to be asked to go on tuck shop duty or make pine cone decorations for the school fete. I have a friend, a female doctor, who secretly confessed she consoles herself when driving to work on days she looks particularly grotty by hoping people may notice the doctor's badge on her car and judge her in that light; *'She's* not at all bad . . . for a doctor.'

The other day I sat in a meeting discussing some business with a very smooth man. I saw him looking at my lap and glancing down I noticed the remains of my breakfast, stuck fast to the hemline. 'Oh you know what these three year olds are like . . . vegemite fingers,' I said, laughing it off. Far better to wear another hat, be the mother for a moment, than have him realise I'm just a slob.

For some of us it takes the pressure off achieving in our jobs. The academic who's just had a paper rejected by a scholarly journal consoles herself with the thought that she did write in during the school holidays, with two of the children suffering from measles. The perfectionist can spread her obsessions around instead of lumping them all on her work or her children.

Often we may achieve more because of our many roles, perhaps in areas which don't receive much recognition. Like being the person everyone in the office talks to about their problems, the listener, the nurturer, the comforter. It's time-consuming stuff extending the mother role into the work situation but can be rewarding. It is just one example of the benefits that come from being different things to different people. Perhaps we have more to give. Certainly as you take on more roles you are forced to move onto a whole new plane of efficiency. Pressure cuts through non-essentials like a knife. I've just watched a friend commence working full-time after raising four children to school age. Previously an immaculate woman smoothly running an elegant house where everything shone and all gadgets worked, she laughs at her rapid slide. 'The house was first to go,' she says. 'I've watched it disintegrate around me, and what's really wonderful is that I don't care. It used to drive me mad when the kitchen fan broke down and I'd frantically arrange to get it fixed. Now I just open the windows instead.' And of course, if you do drop in the house still looks great. She copes with the essentials quickly, efficiently. The rest doesn't matter.

With housework, like so many areas of life, you very swiftly reach the point of maximum return. A whizz through the kitchen, reassigning objects scattered through the house to their rightful place, some fresh flowers thrown in a vase. Just enough to make you feel good. Who needs to suffer the agony of hanging around to watch the first wet dog hit that newly polished floor? All you need is a *long* solid dose of school holidays to realise motherhood is more rewarding in smaller doses. For them and for us. Ask any mother.

Husbands aren't so easy. Most of us have problems cutting down our wifely duties. There's the question of guilt. Those wistful sighs about past times when backs were scrubbed, necks massaged, when you had time to talk. The resigned look when he rolls up his sleeves to hide the lost cuff button, or consigns yet one more odd sock to the growing pile in his drawer. The jeans with the broken fly gather dust on your sewing basket.

Our problem is the fact that often we take it all on by choice and while we gain, our husbands lose. His hassled frantic wife has less time for nurturing, pampering goes by the board. We're too guilty to demand he shares the load. Our working may even cost the family money in paying for childcare and cleaning, holiday camps or whatever. Support systems become expensive.

The good husbands understand and offer to help. 'All you have to do is ask' they say. But even helpful husbands have to be thanked, their contributions acknowledged, credit given. All those pleases and thank yous. Being grateful takes time and energy. It's often easier to do it yourself.

But it's worth it. Superwoman doesn't just mean super drudge. Sam D. Sieber, a sociologist at Columbia University, researched working women a few years ago and found them well aware of the benefits of placing their social eggs in many baskets. They showed him that the more roles they had, the more benefits, not just duties they accrued. Quite simply, more is more. Sieber talks about 'role accumulation' arguing that, for many women, the tension engendered by conflict was totally overshadowed by the rewards of their many roles. With many roles you may be spread thin but you have social security. Should you fail in one role, the others will buffer you. As you acquire more roles, you become more valuable to the people who know you in each role. Because you're valuable and less available, they'll probably slacken their demands on you. 'Getting around' may leave you drained, but neither bored nor boring.

It makes sense, doesn't it? And works most of the time. Our juggling acts give us room to move, lots of strokes from different folks. Of course there are dangers living life inflated like a tyre to a maximum of pressure. Occasionally there's a blow-out, the strain is too great. Sometimes we all long to opt out. But provided we don't believe in our own propaganda, and take the super-woman image too seriously, we can rejoice in taking the best from all our many worlds and avoiding the worst of them.

Superwoman is superb, most of the time.

The Contented Workaholic

You wake up. Yawn, have a good stretch, and realise it's Monday morning. Do you greet the thought with a groan? Well, you're certainly not alone but there *are* some people who rarely, if ever, suffer Mondayitis. Within our midst are individuals who share a secret passion for a part of life most of us usually despise – work.

Work addiction is hardly the sort of thing you boast about. No one wants to be labelled a workaholic. The good news for addicts is there is now evidence that there is such a thing as a *contented* workaholic, a person whose passion for work is seen as a positive creative force in his or her life rather than a push towards self-destruction. American psychologist Marilyn M. Machlowitz has conducted research which shows that not all workaholics are driven by fear of failure or compulsive over-ambition; and that a passion for work *can* contribute rather than detract from fulfilment in other aspects of life. Machlowitz proposes a new category of *contented* workaholics – perhaps we should call them *workaphiles* – people whose zest for work spills over into other areas of their lives, people who are energised by work rather than drained by it. As part of her research on workaholics at Yale University, Machlowitz discovered that people who like their work are more likely to feel satisfied with the rest of their lives; 'Satisfaction with work and with life,' she concluded, 'are more apt to be intertwined than mutually exclusive.'

But with the workaphile, we're not just talking about career *satisfaction* – the attitude of such people to their careers shouldn't be described in such lukewarm terms. The workaphile, is not just *content* with his or her work; rather we are talking about a passion, an obsession, a love of work which leads the workaphile to share many of the quirks, the give-away characteristics of the problem workaholic. In Machlowitz's terms both the workaphile and workaholic are people whose 'desire to work hard and long is intrinsic, whose work habits almost always exceed the prescriptions of the job and the expectations of those with whom and for whom they work.'

On the surface they appear the same – avoiding holidays and social engagements, breaking dates, sneaking briefcases into holiday luggage, packing more books than bikinis. Both the workaholic and workaphile spend most of their waking hours working, tend to blur the distinction between work and play and rarely tune out totally from their work, work anytime, anywhere. These work junkies work long hours but it's not the number of hours that defines their addiction, it's their attitude to work. They don't regard themselves as overworked – work is their obsession, they can't get enough of it. For the work addict, there's never a question of killing time, rather an eternal problem of finding more of it. They tend to sleep less than most people and are constantly seeking means of cramming more into each day. 'Workaholics are racehorses,' said Machlowitz, referring particularly to contented workaholics, 'they're not overworked, they're going at the speed that's best for them. They are extremely energetic and enthusiastic. They'll say things like "If I didn't have to pay the rent, I'd do my job for free", or that their sixteen-hour workday seems only six hours long.'

So the workaphile and problem workaholic share the same passion, and pursue it with similar vigour. But, at least in one case, with the problem workaholic, work obsession frequently leads to disaster. The workaholic burns out when non-stop work and devotion does not produce the expected satisfaction and rewards, health risks increase, and they become prime candidates for high blood pressure, early heart disease, their personal and family life suffers. With the workaphile, the passion for work acts the other way – creating energy, enhancing health and happiness. Workaphiles are obsessed, as their families and friends know only too well, but talking to them there's little sign that their work obsession is anything but a positive force in their lives – and they know how lucky they are.

Is it luck? What separates these contented successful workaphiles from the dangerous world of the workaholic? It was this question which led Marilyn Machlowitz to study workaholics for her doctorate at Yale University. 'I became fascinated,' she said, 'by professors and deans who appeared to work very hard without the unhappiness or narrowness that was supposed to accompany devotion to duty. These observations led me to question the negative stereotype associated with the work "workaholic".' She set out to discover 'what was wrong – and more important, what was right – about being a workaholic.'

Machlowitz came up with four factors to distinguish the 'contented workaholic' (workaphile) from the 'problem workaholic'.

Acceptance (or non acceptance) of their work habits by their families.

Autonomy and variety in their work,

A good (or poor) match between their personal skills and styles, and those required by their jobs, and

Their general state of health.

Leaving aside for the moment the issue of acceptance by families, partners and lovers, it is obvious that the other factors are likely to interact and all be influenced by further considerations such as personality and attitude to work.

For instance, Machlowitz's work shows the problem workaholic exhibits characteristics similar to the Type A personality described by cardiologists Meyer Friedman and Ray Rosenman – excessive competitive drive, intense time urgency, a fierce need for achievement, concern for deadlines, impatience, anger – characteristics which have been shown to contribute to the risk of heart disease. The latest research on Type A behaviour suggests it is anger and even more important, cynicism, which are the crucial emotions which place the Type A personality at risk. The workaphile, on the other hand, perhaps is more likely to fall into a Type B category, showing less urgency, hostility, less time pressure, no excessive competitiveness. Workaphiles are driven not by a fear of failure but a desire to excel, to get the most out of their jobs. They are their *own* slaves – not competing with others, but responding to their own desire for enjoyment and excellence in their chosen careers.

So while the workaphile and workaholic work at the same pace and may experience similar levels of stress, it may be that the workaphile handles the situation differently. Some other research has relevance. Suzanne C. Kobasa, a University of Chicago psychologist, studied a group of business executives and found that only 20 per cent of those under high stress became sick. The majority weathered the storm in perfect health. The healthy ones, says Kobasa, shared three characteristics: the belief that they can control or influence the events in their jobs; an ability to feel deeply involved in or committed to the activities of their lives and an anticipation of change as an exciting challenge to further development.

So the health issue, the way the individual reacts to stress is influenced by his or her attitudes to work and to life, which in turn are influenced by personality. All these factors interact to push one work addict towards the destructive life of the workaholic and another towards the fulfilling life of the workaphile.

Wilfred Jarvis is an Australian psychologist who has had extensive experience in dealing with executives and others in the work place. He agrees there are two types of work addicts; 'the person I call the workaholic is obsessive – compulsive. He or she is on

a treadmill and just can't stop. There's no let up, and more important no *joy* in their work. They are driven by forces they don't
understand to always climb a higher mountain but when they get
there, there's no pleasure, no fulfilment. Workaholism, like alcoholism, to me refers to someone who has taken a course which
is self-destructive, everything they do in the end will injure themselves or someone else in their lives. They have a lot of things
to show – their wealth, their status, power – but when you talk
to them they have no close relationships, no one really loves them
and they don't really love themselves.'

Jarvis believes the factor which really distinguished the
workaholic from the workaphile has to do with self-love, self-
image – what he calls the 'who-ness' scale – private feelings about
self-worth, self-fulfilment, 'who-am-I' type feelings. The workaholic scores highly on the 'what-ness' scale – reflecting public
status, work achievement but ranks low in terms of 'who-ness'.
In the work situation the workaholic's lack of self esteem often
results in destructive emotions: anger, cynicism, suspicion, dis-
trust, precisely the emotions which place his or her health at risk.
The workaphile, high on both 'what-ness' and 'who-ness', is fueled
by quite different emotions and has quite a different attitude to
his work. Jarvis has found it is the workaphile rather than the
workaholic who is least likely to complain about overwork. 'The
workaphile doesn't sit down and say that is work, that is leisure,
work is bad news, leisure is good news, he or she doesn't make
that distinction. Unlike the workaholic who often wears hard
work as a badge or martyrdom – 'look at all the work I'm taking
home this weekend,' 'look at what I'm doing for the company', – for the workaphile, the work is part of life's fulfilment.
I have known workaphiles who are some of the healthiest, most
satisfied people I have ever met – every moment counts, they have
strong personal lives, strong family lives, they do all kinds of
interesting things as well as work, but not at the sacrifice of their
personal lives, their health, and not at the sacrifice of some sense
of obligation to total community.'

For Jarvis, how a person feels about himself and his relationships with other people is the crucial factor in determining whether a work addiction becomes a positive or negative force in a person's life.

Working as an industrial psychologist, Jarvis is all too aware that the workaphile is regarded as an oddity in a country where work is despised; 'Work is bad news for a lot of Australians. Even when someone mentions the word "work", you hear a change of inflection. It's part of our tradition from way back – our Anglo-Saxon, Irish background which is so different from the thinking one finds in America. The work ethic in America . . . "we can all lick this continent by dint of hard work, trust in God and our own hands" . . . that type of thinking is *still* running pretty strongly in the American ethos. I think our origins are unfortunate. We started in the beginning resenting authority, resenting the bondage and I don't think we ever got over that attitude.'

The result is the workaphile finds himself or herself on the outer. As Jarvis says; 'Just as Beethoven is regarded as strange by people who have only heard of chopsticks, the workaphile with a passion for work is rubbished by people who couldn't possibly imagine feeling like that. They say he must be weird, driven by the devil to work like that. It's an experience that unfortunately they can't imagine.'

There's the story of an Australian studying at Harvard who found there was a real difference in attitudes to work amongst his fellow students. All the Americans used to leave their lights on at night so that it would look as if they were working late even if they weren't. The Australians? They turned their lights off or right down low so that no one could tell if they *were* working hard.

In such a culture, it is hardly surprising that the workaphile may at times feel guilty, or odd. Work addicts are aware that their passion is incomprehensible to the non-addicted. People who work to live cannot understand those who live to work, and love it. So the workaphile is constantly ragged by people wanting him or her to pursue what they see as a well-rounded, balanced, more normal life. You are not supposed to *want* to work in the evenings or at weekends. These times are to be spent with family, friends, pursuing hobbies. Every beauty competition contestant can reel off half a dozen hobbies, from basket weaving to opera singing. Yet the workaphile would often be pushed to list one consuming leisure activity, one absorbing hobby. As playwright Neil Simon said, 'I wish I *could* do other things well besides write . . . play an instrument, learn other languages, cook, ski. My greatest sense of accomplishment is that I didn't waste time *trying* to learn those things.'

When work is your greatest pleasure, should you be forced to spend time pursuing other activities? The most annoying thing for the non-workaphile is that work addiction is liable to lead to a successful career. As someone once said – workaholism is the one clean way to the top. Because of this the work junkies are sure to attract criticism and perhaps envy from others who regard their own work with less enthusiasm. There are exceptions. Marilyn Machlowitz mentions running into a young mathematician who responded eagerly on discovering she was writing a book on workaholics – 'Will it tell me how to become one?', was his question.

It is the reaction of others in the work situation, to his or her work habits which makes it crucial the workaphile find a career which allows some autonomy. Workaphiles often run into trouble in bureaucracies where their sixteen-hour days are unlikely to endear them to colleagues who have settled into less strenuous work patterns. Equally infuriating is the workaphile's attitude to the trappings of success . . . money, status etc. Since the essence of work addiction is the *intrinsic* enjoyment, most workaphiles have no doubt they would continue to work as hard for less money and less status. It was fascinating how often the workaphiles I spoke to mentioned the fact that they were well aware that it was the taxation system which benefited most from their extra efforts. But generally it wasn't seen as a problem. Gerald Stone, producer of 'Sixty Minutes' commented; 'I'm amazed to hear people say that if they just keep taxing us, we just won't work, what's the point in working etc. To me, the rewards are in doing the job, enjoying the work not just money and status. Sure it's nice to enjoy the benefits . . . to be able to buy a nice suit, eat in a restaurant but if someone said, "Right, from now on your tax will be 98 per cent", it wouldn't stop me. But for someone working on a factory line, it must be different. *They* are the people who deserve more money.'

Unfashionable attitudes – and when they are coupled with the workaholics energy and enthusiasm, – it's hardly surprising these people aren't always the easiest people to work with or work for. As Machlowitz puts it: 'They march to the tune of a different stopwatch' and while all around are passing out with fatigue, they are eager to press on.

Crazy, eh? But the interesting thing about the workaphiles I talked to is that their energy and enthusiasm often does seem to inspire others and their weird habits are frequently regarded with affection rather than resentment by those around them. When interviewing workaphiles, every now and then I see their eyes glaze and these eager minds would drift off to some other pressing matter, some other idea. It's no wonder that workaphiles are constantly in trouble with friends, family and lovers for thinking about work at inappropriate moments! These are hardly the sort of people you'd want on a fishing trip, a Pacific Island cruise.

Their idea of relaxation is often an activity, a sport so competitive and mentally and physically strenuous that they are forced to concentrate on something other than work. Many try to avoid holidays and, when forced into them, take a long time to slow down and are soon eager to return. Their friends are forced to be tolerant of broken engagements and forgotten social events.

Which brings us to the crunch . . . the work junky may well be happy with his habit, but it isn't always as easy finding others prepared to live with and share his addiction. Machlowitz found it's often the people who live with the workaphile who pay the price for his or her obsession. As the saying goes: 'If you choose work to be your lover, you'll have trouble with your wife'. Perhaps we should add . . . and children, and friends. Golda Meir was interviewed by the *New York Times* not long before her death; 'Somebody said I was married to my job,' she remarked, 'My children suffered at various times, but when they got older, they understood. As for my husband, he was a wonderful human being. Bad luck he married me.'

For men and women it *is* bad luck when they discover they are married to a workaphile, particularly if they assume that marriage will cure their partner of the addiction. (Workaphiles rarely change, and there's little point looking forward to his or her retirement from the work scene. As Margaret Mead once said; 'I may die – but I'll never retire' – and most workaphiles share her sentiments.) The workaphile has already found the love of his or her life and accepting you come second in line isn't always easy. There are plenty of marriages which founder as a result of the inherent tensions in such a relationship. Yet Wilfred Jarvis finds that many of the workaphiles he has met have successful marriages. 'I know many who have rich relationships with other people and good marriages but those marriages require a great deal of reciprocal understanding. With the men, most I am thinking about have wives who are very fulfilled in their own professions or who get a tremendous kick out of raising a family. Once the kids are grown up they often go back to work, or do something else. These women are people who *matter* in the community – and hence they don't feel they need to compete with their husband's work. The couple don't want to possess each other – they each have their own areas of achievement and fulfilment.'

Since the relationships issue featured so strongly in Machlowitz's research, I talked not only to workaphiles but also to their wives and husbands about the effects of work addiction on a marriage. Naturally the couples most willing to talk were those who have found a solution to the relationship problem and often the best way out seems to be for the workaphile to find someone else who shares his addiction, or at least someone who has tasted a similar passion. These couples often end up with amazingly complex lives, as they juggle their respective commitments but there's usually less resentment, and often great pleasure in witnessing each other's highs. Then there are the more traditional relationships where one partner plays a more supportive role, nurturing the addict, under-standing his or her need without sharing the same obsession. Sometimes the supporter will be a husband, but more often the role falls to the wife, and it's a situation which requires incredi-ble patience and flexibility. Not that it is necessary for a workaphile to work outside the home – there have always been plenty of women who have attacked their roles as housewife and mother with similar addiction and energy. The tireless mother who sews clown outfits for her children's fete far into the night, the woman who cleans her bathroom tiles with a toothbrush – these are the invisible workaphiles whose skills are so often undervalued and whose obsession brings less certain or tangible rewards.

As a potential workaphile whose addiction has long been curbed by the demands of motherhood, it was fascinating for me to talk to other mothers about the problem of feeding one's habit midst the joys and demands of raising children. We all worry about the effects on the children of growing up with mums who secretly welcome a school detention as a chance for an extra hour of work or sit glazed-eyed through school concerts, clapping mechanically, minds elsewhere plotting and planning.

Machlowitz finds that growing up with a work-addicted par-ent can push children in either direction – they become carbon copies or beach bums. Presumably much depends on how your other parent reacted to the workaphile's habits – where it is the cause of much family strife and resentment, it is hardly surpris-ing that some children decide to opt out of the work ethic altogether. But as Wilfred Jarvis points out, sometimes the worka-phile's energy and enthusiasm spills over to his children; 'Lots of children of workaholics say to me, "I am not going to be like my father". But most of the children of workaphiles say, "Gee, I admire my dad" and most of these kids turn out pretty well . . . Not necessarily in terms of great achievement of status but as healthy, normal human beings.'

Contented workaholics breeding other contented workaholics. Some would say it's just what this country needs. But for the moment, there are unfortunately all too few of them around.

Perhaps it's just that in a nation obsessed by flexitime and shorter hours, they are afraid of showing their true colours. Machlowitz found them everywhere – in every occupation, white collar, blue collar, even suffering amongst the present unemployed. Perhaps giving them a new, brighter label, calling them 'workaphile' instead of the tainted 'workaholic' will draw them out. Force them out of the closet. Here's hoping.

Men and Health

Helpless Men

*I*t's not that I avoid discussing female health issues. I've spent months on end wallowing in vaginal diseases and post-menopausal symptoms, my bookshelves are weighed down with text after text on gynaecological problems, self-help female health care pamphlets, books on PMT, cystitis, breast cancer, menopause, menstruation. You name it, we've had it and I've talked about it.

But men are different. The true-blue pie-eating Aussie bloke still regards it as rather suspect to show too much interest in health and keeping fit. Males shuffle reluctantly into the doctor's surgery . . . 'My wife insisted I check this out, you know how women like to fuss.'

Male patients see predominantly male doctors who often conspire with them to maintain the myth that real men don't feel pain or anxiety or depression, the stiff-upper lip tradition that encourages men to ignore physical symptoms and stifle emotional distress. Women are permitted to be dependent, to seek help and are far more likely to be given it. Faced with a man and a woman with equivalent symptoms of anxiety, high blood pressure or whatever, research evidence shows it is the woman who is far more likely to be receiving treatment. Yes, it *is* true that often that treatment may be inappropriate, valium to obliterate the tedium of housework or sleeping pills to wipe out the stress of the day. But a need is recognised rather than ignored.

Many males are lucky enough to spend much of their lives avoiding doctors and acquiring minimum knowledge of their bodies and health care issues. But the woman's reproductive system forces her to acquire more knowledge about how her body works. The healthy woman visits doctors for contraception, for having babies, for maintaining and adjusting her menstrual cycle, for menopause and the innumerable problems which can develop in her complicated plumbing. It's a nuisance, but ultimately many women end up better equipped to deal with more serious health problems which may develop.

Used to being poked and prodded, used to talking about their bodies and their emotions, the female patient may cope better or at least be willing to admit she's in trouble. For the male, the stress of illness, the embarrassment of examinations, the uncomfortable dependency is often harder to acknowledge and harder to handle.

And when he's feeling vulnerable or scared or nervous, who can he talk to – his mates? The man feeling under threat through the ordeal of infertility tests is hardly likely to discuss his feelings with other, presumably fertile friends, whereas the woman uses the support and comfort of friends to survive such experiences. The man who shrinks from looking and touching the body of his wife after a mastectomy – hides his guilt and retreats from her, and from his own feelings.

When faced with impossible situations women break down. Usually someone notices and is there to pick up the pieces. Men break out, sometimes using alcohol to drown out the world, sometimes releasing bursts of emotions behind the wheel of a car or slamming a squash ball into the wall. Being seen as the fragile sex protects women and ultimately contributes to their strength. Males are left vulnerable, running risks with their health, their sexuality and ultimately their lives through their attempts to maintain a facade of masculinity.

Masculinity is a Health Hazard

Masculinity is a health hazard. To be a man is to be at risk, to take risks with life, risks with health, risks which kill. Our men die younger. Females outlive them by up to seven years and the gap is widening. Masculinity pays a price. Emotional words? Yes, but it's not an issue I can be dispassionate about. It's too near to home.

My first husband Dennis died – aged thirty-seven. A heart attack killed him, so they said. The medical explanation, clean and clinical, but the real reason? A life as a journalist: ambitions, competition, tension, travelling, deadlines . . . mainlining adrenalin; too close to disasters, danger even, too much excitement; an ulcer in his twenties, heavy smoker, drinking . . . the typical 'journo' and a recipe for disaster. Then he dropped out, to help me publish a magazine. Finally a calmer life, responsibilities shared, not shouldered alone. But he had learned too well to act like a man, kept financial worries to himself, adding figures in his sleep – and told me not to worry. So the blood pressure was still high, the warning signals still there. Then came a five-hour emergency operation to repair a ruptured bowel – an intestine ravaged by diverticulitis. It's a disease they believe is contributed to by poor diet. Never one for health foods, my macho man would joke about alfalfa eaters and leave vegetables untouched. His favourite food? Chip sandwiches. And I indulged him, sometimes.

The operation was touch-and-go but he survived. Yet for him the results were horrific. He had a temporary colostomy, a bag leading from the intestine, storing waste to give his ravaged bowel time to heal. An ordeal for anyone, the odour, the messiness, embarrassment . . . but worse, perhaps, for a man unused to medical examinations, unused to the indignity, the poking and prodding and particularly the anal examinations; a man, like most men, whose contact with doctors had been minimal. Now his injured body exposed him abruptly to the medical world where there's no room for squeamishness or embarrassment. His privacy was invaded. I watched his tension grow. He couldn't cope with being so vulnerable.

There must be reasons why a man should die of heart failure the day before they were to remove the colostomy bag, the day before he was to be rid of his torment. Lifestyle? Too many beers? Too much smoking? Too little exercise? The stress of illness? It all added up to being a typical male. That's what killed him. So, on this issue I'm far from a fence-sitter.

There are facts – plenty of them to prove that men die younger, that when the crunch comes, we're the stronger sex. An Australian girl born before 1910 could have expected to outlive her male playmates by about 3.6 years. Now the gap has widened to over seven years. In 1981 statistics showed that the Australian male life expectancy was 71.38 years, and female life expectancy 78.42 years.

Most of the diseases that kill us affect both men and women. The hazard of being male is that men develop these diseases more often and earlier than we do, and are more likely to die of them at an early age. So while we all tend to die of the same things in the end – cancer, heart attacks, strokes, respiratory diseases – many more men die in their forties and fifties while most women hang in there until their sixties, seventies and even eighties.

It's not hard to prove that much of this difference is due to lifestyle. For every panting jogger who starts his day with muesli, there are still hundreds of Aussie blokes enjoying the good life . . . too much booze, cigarettes, bad diet, no exercise.

It's not part of the image of the all-Aussie male to be concerned about health issues. 'She'll be right, mate,' he says reaching out for another beer before staggering out to drive himself home. The chain-smoking executive finds another means of killing himself . . . overdosing on stress, the heavy business lunch, that extra martini.

Sure, there are plenty of women moving into the same territory, adopting similar lifestyles and smoking to help them cope. But however much we women endanger ourselves through lifestyle changes, it appears men have a self-destructive edge. Their behaviour apart, there seems to be an extra male factor which places men at risk, inherited from their genes. Or is it a female factor, female hormones which protect us and make us less susceptible to the diseases which cause men to die much earlier?

It's a complex issue and to really understand why differences exist we have to compare male and female mortality rates at different ages. Starting with young men, we find the male/female difference in mortality rates takes a sudden leap from late teens onwards. What's happened? He's got wheels! Accidents, particularly car accidents, are the most common cause of death of young men. A male is two-and-a-half times more likely to be killed in an accident than a female – sporting accidents, occupational accidents – but mainly car accidents. It's not just that men drive more than women – even when that difference is evened out, the male behind the wheel is still more at risk. As we all know, sometimes it's the demon alcohol at work. In Australia it has been estimated that roughly one-half of all traffic fatalities, and about 80 per cent of these at ages fifteen to twenty-four can be attributed directly to the misuse of alcohol, especially amongst males. Sober or not, men drive differently from women, there's research to prove it. All too often the car becomes a weapon in the competition against other men. This time the risk is a lot greater than banging heads on a football field (but that too can kill).

Male driving habits are now one of the main reasons why men die younger than women. If we look back over the past forty years we find that male life expectancy has remained fairly stable. Our men have managed to wipe out the benefits both men and women experienced from the late 1940s onwards, due to advances in medical science – antibiotics, penicillin and the like – and the virtual elimination of infectious diseases, particularly tuberculosis, as a major cause of death. From the 1950s, women started living longer; men would have shown similar benefits . . . but they blew it.

It was not just that they discovered the motor car, they acquired another fatal habit . . . smoking cigarettes. Males smoke more than women – for every two women smokers there are three men smokers. There is now no doubt that this is *the* factor that accounts for the male/female difference in mortality rate in the mid years, particularly the forties and fifties. The evidence is now overwhelming that smoking is linked to the major killer diseases of our time – cardiovascular diseases and cancer.

Research studies from all major Western countries have shown that men's higher cigarette consumption is the major reason men die younger from heart disease. The effect of cigarettes far outweighs all the other factors which may contribute to heart disease. So it's male behaviour – male habits – which place them most at risk, but there are other factors operating. Even among non-smokers, men have a higher rate of fatal coronary heart disease than females, which suggests a sex difference that may have more to do with the way men are made than the way they behave. There has been some fascinating research attempting to pin down possible genetic factors to account for males' higher risk, and the evidence so far points to the role of hormones.

If we compare men and women of different ages we find male death rate through heart attack is always higher than the female's until the seventies when we just about catch up. This suggests that while female hormones are present, we're given some protection which could then gradually drop off after menopause. Research shows women who have had both ovaries removed show an increased risk of heart disease. Early menopause seems also to be associated with increased risk.

It's not only a question of hormones – that's only the beginning. As we've all been taught, other aspects of our lifestyle appear to contribute to cardiovascular diseases . . . diet, particularly cholesterol intake, stress, exercise and fitness. Are there differences between men and women in the way we look after ourselves and our bodies?

Well, it's very difficult to assess relative fitness of males and females and it's something which has recently undergone significant changes. There's no doubt that men used to be fitter in the days when their occupations often involved manual labour. But that's changed. A National Heart Foundation study on heart risk factors showed there was little difference between men and women in the amount of physical exertion involved in their work, but more men than women play sport or are involved in keep-fit activities. Sixteen per cent of men and 9 per cent of women practised the recommended three times per week regular vigorous exercise required for cardiovascular fitness.

So, in theory, men are making more effort to keep fit. Yet looking around me in my mixed aerobic exercise classes, it's obvious the recent boom in attendance is still mainly female with a sprinkling of young men. The rise in popularity of such exercise classes is quite recent and has occurred since the 1980 National Heart Foundation Study. Fitness patterns may be changing rapidly.

Then there's diet, and here too there are sex differences. The risk study found women eat less butter, fewer eggs and less fat on their meat than men, and add less salt to their meals. Have those endless articles on weight-loss diets and nutrition in women's magazines sunk in? Or is it simply that women don't have time to sit down and eat eggs for breakfast because they are too busy cooking them for other people?

Twice as many women (12 per cent) as men in the Heart Foundation Study were on diets to control weight and it paid off . . . a little. The risk study found a noticeable increase in male obesity over forty. Forty-eight per cent of men over the age of thirty-five were overweight or obese, compared with 42 per cent of women over the age of forty. Adult females are much slimmer than women of fifty years ago but men tend to be fatter than their grandfathers were.

All this doesn't count for much compared with another major difference in male/female diet – alcohol consumption. Male drinking habits place them very much more at risk. The Heart Foundation Study found 40 per cent of men in the forty-five to fifty-nine-year age range drank alcohol on five or more days per week. The proportion of regular women drinkers increased to 20 per cent at the age of thirty-five years, after which it remained fairly constant. Cancer, the second of the killer diseases, strikes many more males than females. Lung cancer obviously accounts for much of the difference and we know about the link here with cigarette smoking. But male behaviour also increases the risk of cancer of the oesophagus – a cancer which has increased since 1950 in parallel with the increase in male alcohol consumption. Rectal cancer and pancreatic cancer are also associated with alcohol usage. In 50 per cent of deaths caused by cirrhosis of the liver, alcohol is implicated. Here, too, males are paying the price for their excessive drinking . . . and this is despite the fact that the female liver is more susceptible to alcohol.

Cancer accounts for about one fifth of the difference in life expectancy between the sexes, and 70 per cent of that is due to lung cancer.

In the past women have had an advantage in surviving cancer. The principle female site of cancer has been the breast which is far more accessible to treatment than the male's major target area – the lung. Breast cancer has a significantly higher survival rate than lung cancer. But patterns are changing. As we all know, more young women are now smoking, and this is greatly increasing the female risk of lung cancer. Just recently lung cancer overtook breast as the major female cancer site and more women will die young as a result.

Just when men are taking the hint and changing their habits, women are making it harder on themselves. In the late 1940s, 70 per cent of males smoked. By 1983 the figure had dropped to 37 per cent. Males of all ages are giving up smoking. Older women show a similar pattern but since more young women have taken up the habit, the overall female rate in the same period has only dropped from 32 to 30 per cent. But in terms of the effects on male/female difference in life expectancy we won't expect to see much change for many years. These things take time and besides, so much else is happening.

For instance, since 1967 there has been an overall drop of 40 per cent in heart attack deaths. This is an extraordinary development which is causing much excitement among health care professionals. It could be related to changed smoking habits but since the drop applies to both men and women, that can't explain this huge difference in both sexes.

Better medical treatment for hypertension may have contributed to the drop in mortality, or perhaps some of the answer lies in the new coronary care units to treat heart attack victims. Then there are all the changes in diet and exercise patterns I've already talked about . . .

A study by the Human Population Laboratory, in California, compared men and women on various lifestyle measures and related this to the mortality rate of the participants over a nine-and-a-half-year period. They looked at smoking, exercise patterns, alcohol intake, weight, eating and sleeping habits. The study found the health practices particularly affected male mortality. Men who did all the right things had a mortality rate of 62 per cent less than that of men who only practised a few of the recommended health procedures. In females healthy habits only produced a 43 per cent difference.

The results suggest men have even more to gain by changing their habits . . . but will they do it? A walk around a crowded summer beach makes you wonder. They lie there, beer bellies bulging in the sun, their bright-red noses veined by years of elbow-bending. Still unaware, unashamed?

The masculine role makes it hard for men to admit they may be vulnerable and in need of health care. Doctors tell me male patients come in reluctantly to complain of this or that and are still afraid of being seen as 'sissy' by making a fuss. 'I didn't want to come but my wife insisted.'

A survey by the Royal Australian College of General Practitioners, in Sydney, found that of approximately 4,000 consultations, 40 per cent were male patients. Some of the difference is accounted for by the fact that healthy women see doctors for contraception, ante-natal visits, etc. We're not all sick. But when males and females have the same medical problem, it's more likely to be the female who seeks and receives treatment. For instance, the Heart Foundation Study showed that only 33 per cent of males compared with 61 per cent of females found to have hypertension were on treatment for high blood pressure.

Perhaps women are more aware of health issues as a result of media promotion – magazine articles, daytime television programmes which forcefeed us information about diet and health. But there's another difference . . . our reproductive system. What is called 'the curse', our monthly menstrual cycle, sets us up from mid-teens onwards for a lifetime of potential problems, all requiring medical care and consultation. It's a complex system, so crucial to our fertility and our overall health and there's much that can go wrong. These female experiences are so complex they require an expert to care for them – a gynaecologist. This specialised medical service provides us with a safeguard, for while caring for our health, the gynaecologist, or even the GP, will often pick up things which go wrong elsewhere. For instance, doctors routinely test blood pressure before prescribing the contraceptive pill, and while monitoring pregnancy. Diabetes and kidney disease are often detected through urine tests during pregnancy. The doctor's expertise and our female need for supervision; the combination protects us and, often, may help us to overcome our squeamishness or embarrassment about physical examinations.

Of course, as women, we're used to dependency, allowed to admit to vulnerability, expected to seek help. For men it's different, not only as patients but as doctors. One doctor I spoke to mentioned the fact that the male doctor may find it easier to focus on female problems and ignore lifestyle-related illnesses in his male patients, because he probably suffers the same complaints and takes the same risks. The male doctor's own attitudes may also influence another aspect of male health care. Look at cancer of the rectum, the prostate, the lower bowel – the first hint of these diseases may come through an anal examination, a procedure which all too often is neither offered by the male doctor, nor asked for by male patients. Anal examinations should be part of all major male physical examinations. There's a saying in medical circles: 'If you don't put your finger in, you'll put your foot in.' Yet anal examinations are often avoided.

Things are changing . . . gradually. At a urology conference in the United States some time ago, the doctors were asked how many had regular anal examinations. Half the medical audience raised their hands. The doctor who told me this story said he doubted if you'd get more than a handful at a similar conference in this country.

It's not that these cancers are all that common, but early detection can help. The same applies to cancer of the testicles, and moves are afoot in the United States to teach men TSE (Testicle-Self-Examination), so, like women, they can detect lumps early, before the damage spreads.

These are minor problems, rare killers, but they all add up . . . to a case of neglect. An increasing waste of male lives, particularly older males, through crazy masculine behaviour. As far as I'm concerned the male, the older male, is an endangered species which is well worth protecting. Let's help them try to mend their ways. We'll probably still outlast them, but at least there will be a few more to go around when we need them most.

Executive Sex

One of my favourite cartoons shows a rather pompous-looking businessman type in bed with a disgruntled-looking young woman. 'Of course I ejaculate prematurely,' he says. 'I'm a very busy man.'

A bit close to the bone? Well, all you busy men, perhaps it's time you realised that, however skilled your boardroom manoeuvring, your bedroom performance may not be quite up to scratch. In fact, in these increasingly troubled times, with high interest rates and international recession, it is not only business confidence which is being undermined. The sexual performance of the average Australian businessman is also in danger of entering a recession. More males are finding their sexual relationships crumbling under the strain busy lives impose on physical and sexual health. And although the economy may recover, their bodies and their sexuality may not.

To lay it on the line . . . suppose I am in the market for a husband/lover. I seek a solid long-term future investment, a reasonably regular service agreement and some guarantee against major equipment failure. Would I turn to the local business community to find such a commodity? Never!

The everyday life of the businessman exposes him to a whole range of sexual problems. Businessmen pop up all over the sex therapy literature. The middle-level executive who is passed over for promotion and suddenly finds himself impotent with his wife. The suburban middle-aged bank manager who beds his blonde secretary as a boost to his flagging ego and can't ejaculate. The obese, heavy-smoking forty-five-year-old accountant whose wife complains is never interested in sex. The tense money-market man who ejaculates prematurely. Different jobs but similar stresses and equally disastrous effects on sexual relationships.

I mention the age of many of these fading Don Juans because such problems do tend to occur more in older men. This need not be the case – you should be able to function just as well about as well at seventy as you did at twenty-seven – but lifestyle and expectations play havoc with the sexuality of older men in our society.

Many males expect their sexual performance to suffer with age and this then becomes a self-fulfilling prophecy when they panic at the first sign of a change in sexual functioning. Anxiety is the classic sexual killer. More important, however, is the relationship between physical and sexual health. We will have to see a lot more fit, healthy middle-aged men before we can expect men's sexual performance *not* to decline with age.

Before explaining this relationship between physical and sexual health more fully, a few words about what is normal sexual performance. Sexual pleasure is a variable feast and I cannot tell you how a good or even average Australian businessman would or should behave in bed. It doesn't matter how often you have sex or how many positions you use . . . what matters is whether you enjoy it and whether or not you give pleasure to your partner. It's pretty hard to do either of these if you are worried about having an erection or ejaculating too soon.

In case you think I am giving males a hard time, I must also point out that female executives, women in the work force, run similar risks of damaging their sexual and emotional relationships. There is not yet much research on effects of work pressure on women's physical and sexual health. However, I suspect we will find male sexual health is more vulnerable to such stresses. The complexity of the wondrous mechanism underlying male sexual functioning makes it all too easy to throw a spanner in the works.

But what is it about the life of the businessman that places him so much at risk? The most obvious answer is stress.

Tension, stress, anxiety . . . in these days of labour problems, union picketing, financial restrictions, it is a rare businessman who remains unaffected by stress or tension. And if you battle day to day with problems, it's difficult to leave your cares in the office where they belong . . . all too often they end up carrying over into the bedroom with disastrous results.

Tension still rates as the number one cause of male sexual problems. Until recently a figure of 90 per cent of sexual problems was attributed to a psychological cause such as anxiety or tension, with 10 per cent having some physical cause. Recent research has suggested these figures need reassessment.

It is now estimated that perhaps 40 or 50 per cent of some sexual problems have a physical basis and the rest are psychological, or tension-related. But this change in thinking does nothing to exonerate stress as a culprit in male sexual problems.

Specifically, we are seeing an increase in problems of impotence and delayed ejaculation in males suffering from stress-related ailments like high blood pressure, ulcers, heart disease and arteriosclerosis.

Where stress or tension is the direct cause of the sexual problem, there are three major effects on male sexuality. Most commonly, tension causes difficulty in controlling ejaculation or in gaining or maintaining an erection. Occasionally the male will have difficulty reaching a climax and ejaculating – what is known as 'retarded or delayed ejaculation'.

Our knowledge of sexual physiology has not yet provided answers as to how exactly tension or stress affects ejaculation. However, we know it has three main effects on male erection. Firstly, fear or nervousness triggers the body's 'fight-or-flight' reflex which directs blood away from the genital area into the muscles in the arm and legs and to the brain. As erection depends on the amount of blood contained in the internal spongy tissues of the penis, erection cannot occur when the body is tensed for action.

Stress also causes the body to release adrenalin which heightens energy and contracts the penile arteries which must expand for erection to occur. Finally it depresses the level of testosterone in the blood which may add to erection difficulties. So if you carry your work pressures home with you, it's hardly surprising that your body doesn't always behave exactly as you would like it to.

But that's just the immediate effect of stress. If you are a classic workaholic battling daily with work pressures, you are probably indirectly affecting any future career as a Cassanova through deleterious effects on your general health. You have probably heard of the work of cardiologists Meyer Friedman and Ray Rosenman who coined the phrase 'Type A' personality to describe the behaviour of the classic problem workaholic. The Type A individual, with his excessive competitive drive and intense time urgency, is seven times more likely to develop heart disease than his calmer Type B colleague. Heart disease need *not* affect your sexual performance but fear of a heart attack doesn't exactly encourage the relaxation required for easy erection.

Associated illnesses do have a more direct effect. Arteriosclerosis, the buildup of fatty plaque deposits on artery walls, may impair erection. In addition to raising blood pressure, the decreased blood volume in plaque-clogged arteries may interfere with the penis' blood supply during erection.

Then there is high blood pressure – another stress-related disease which can affect erectile ability. Even if it doesn't do so directly, the medical treatments frequently prescribed for this executive condition may also be hitting below the belt. Many of the drugs used to treat high blood pressure (Clonidine, Methyldopa) cause impotence in some males. There are alternative medications available, so before accepting the treatment your doctor prescribes ask him if his wife would want *him* to take it.

Some drugs used to treat severe depression can have the same effect. Depression is a common complaint among pressured high-salaried males, particularly when they hit the painful middle years sometimes known as 'the male menopause'. A career setback, a business reversal, criticism by a boss; it's not hard for a man to find his confidence undermined, the first seeds of self doubt. Now put this man in bed with his wife after a long, tiring day, a few beers on the way home. He reaches over for the comfort of familiar sex and surprise, surprise. His body is also feeling the effects of that long and stressful day and goes on strike.

This pattern may start as the occasional case of erection failure but can lead to a more serious problem as the male becomes anxious about sexual performance. The vicious circle – failure leading to anxiety which leads to repeated failure – is the classic pattern underlying most psychologically-based male sexual problems. Sometimes, instead of loss of erection, the difficulty will be early ejaculation or inability to climax.

When the problem is simply due to anxiety, and the man has a co-operative partner, it is possible through therapy to break this vicious circle and teach the man to learn to respond again.

Continued excessive use of alcohol is often associated with impotence. The toxic effects of alcohol have been shown to cause the liver to create inordinately high levels of an enzyme that destroys testosterone, the male sex hormone which is crucial for maintenance of normal masculine characteristics. Of course, the occasional drink on the way home from work or beer in front of the TV will not have such drastic effects. However, there is a very fine line between the level of alcohol required to cause relaxation and release of inhibitions and the amount needed to interfere with sexual performance. Step over that line a little too often and you may well find yourself with a permanent sexual hangover.

Then there is that other malady which inflicts all you hard-working men – fatigue. From the female point of view, there isn't much point embarking on a sensuous lovemaking session if you know your partner is likely to nod off just when you are halfway up Everest.

I should also mention smoking . . . all those filled ashtrays at board meetings aren't only affecting your heart and your lungs. Smoking has been shown to cause constriction of the arteries which supply blood to the penis. Heavy smokers run a greatly increased risk of future erection problems.

I should also mention the accumulating evidence that males are placing themselves increasingly at risk of death through such horrors as cancer of the testicles, prostate, colon and rectum by avoiding regular medical check-ups. When was the last time you fitted a routine medical examination into your busy appointment schedule?

But perhaps it is time I said a few words about the other vital component in a successful sex life . . . a contented wife or lover. Before getting down to what goes on in the bedroom it should be noted that the problem with being married to a high-powered executive is the loving wife never sees him. A daily dose of resentment and anger isn't exactly foreplay. Plus it's very hard to tell a high-powered superachieving male that much as you admire his business acumen, his bedroom antics don't do much for you at all.

Your relationship with your partner is absolutely vital because if you have a psychologically-induced sexual problem, it is virtually impossible to treat it unless you have a good relationship with a partner who is willing to work through a course of therapy with you. A bad relationship can cause a sexual problem, a good relationship is essential to treat it.

If, however, you have allowed your physical health to affect your sexual functioning, sex therapy may have little to offer. Surgical techniques have been developed to provide various forms of artificial erection through penile splints . . . but you are far better off with the real thing functioning as it should. The complex interaction of nerves, muscles, blood supply and hormones which control male sexual functioning provides hundreds of alternative potential disaster areas. Once you have damaged your penile arteries, for instance, it is unlikely that medical science will ever be able to return to you the gift of normal erection.

So the point which must be emphasised is that it is no use banking on a cure. It's time more men started looking carefully at their lifestyles and concentrating on the prevention of sexual problems. Unfortunately, the average Aussie executive seems hell bent on destroying one of life's great assets . . . and probably won't even realise it's gone until he finds himself the object of a take-over bid or else she calls in the liquidator.

Impotence

Impotence. It used to be so simple. From the sex therapist's point of view, ten years ago impotence was a problem which was mainly due to anxiety, and fear of failure – psychological difficulties which although not easy to treat, at least were quite straightforward. Now impotence is fast emerging as *the* most complex of all the sexual problems, often involving an intricate combination of psychological and physical factors, some of which are permanent and incurable.

Research in Europe, the United States and Australia shows that perhaps 40 to 50 per cent of erectile problems are, at least in part, contributed to by physical causes. The news has revolutionised the approach to both diagnosis and treatment of impotence and left sex therapists floundering. The tragedy is that thousands of men spend years and thousands of dollars receiving totally inappropriate treatment.

Perhaps one in four Australian men over forty experience some erectile problem – frequently as a side effect to some other physical condition, sometimes as the sole complaint. Still a source of shame and embarrassment, impotence usually is revealed reluctantly in the doctor's surgery.

At thirty-two Bob had a car accident. He broke the odd rib, fractured a leg and ruptured his urethra. All healed but he was left impotent. A number of visits to his general practitioner resulted in a course of injections of testosterone, a male hormone used commonly to attempt to treat erectile problems. No result. Bob persevered and was referred to two urologists and one psychiatrist. Tests were conducted. Some new diagnostic techniques were applied. A pressure gauge attached to his penis showed normal tumescence. He was pronounced physically normal – the problem was in his mind. The specialists advised Bob not to worry and the problem might go away.

Two years later, Bob consulted a leading Sydney sex therapist who referred him to a vascular surgeon. Finally the cause was revealed: damage to one of the penile arteries. Vascular surgery is being considered.

The surgeon who discovered Bob's problem works at the vascular unit at Sydney's Royal North Shore Hospital. This unit, the only one of its kind in Australia, has developed some of the diagnostic techniques which are beginning to unravel the mysteries of male erectile function.

Research by the unit has shown that more than 30 per cent of erectile dysfunction is related significantly to vascular problems – the supply of blood to and from the penis. Of 267 patients studied by the unit, eighty-three had a significant problem with their genital vascular system. The most important finding was that 43 per cent of these men showed no other sign of vascular problem – the blood flow difficulties were confined to specific arteries supplying blood to the penis.

From the diagnostic point of view, this means that it cannot be assumed that a man suffering none of the common diseases affecting blood flow – arteriosclerosis or diabetes – is clear of such problems in his pelvic area. Obstructions can occur in the penile blood flow while all other systems are flowing freely.

Many problems involve the inflow of blood to the penis through a number of large arteries and a network of smaller vessels. Occasionally blood can leak from the *corpora cavernosa*, the spongy bodies which inflate to swell the penis into erection. There also can be failures in the outflow system, the veins which allow blood to leave the penis.

Apart from the men whose vascular problems were confined to the genital area, the Royal North Shore unit found a significant percentage of penile blood-flow problems did occur as a consequence of diseases affecting general blood flow.

Of the eighty-three men with penile vascular problems, 25 per cent were found to have diseases affecting small blood vessels, such as diabetes, hypertension and polyendarteritis. Nineteen percent had diseases affecting large blood vessels, such as arteriosclerosis – hardening or thickening of the walls of the arteries which prevents free passage of the blood. The long, well-hidden arteries to the penis are particularly subject to arteriosclerosis and some cases of impotence in young men have been due to a specific form of arteriosclerosis which appears to affect the penile arteries early.

The final group of vascular erectile problems result from some trauma to the pubic area – a car accident or sporting accident, perhaps – causing damage or tearing of blood vessels. The Royal North Shore research points to the need for careful review of the medical history of any man with an erectile dysfunction. Any hint of a vascular problem must be investigated thoroughly. When no such evidence exists, specialists believe it is worthwhile trying sex therapy – the behaviour therapy techniques which can be quite effective with anxiety-produced impotence. If that treatment is unsuccessful, further medical investigation is called for, searching for specific genital vascular problems and other physical problems.

Australian therapists generally are not in favor of leaping too early into unnecessary, expensive medical tests. Derek Richardson, president of the Australian Society of Sex Educators, Researchers and Therapists, suggests a more cautious approach: 'Obviously, careful diagnostic tests are called for if the medical history reveals a potential physical problem but since these can cost up to $2,000 it is foolish not to try behaviour therapy first when medically all seems clear. If that fails, then you must look again and that's where the new diagnostic tests are essential.'

Therein lies a major difficulty. Very few places in Australia have the diagnostic tools to sort out the relative contributions of possible physical and psychological causes of impotence, let alone to track down the specific site of intricate blood-flow problems. Without specialised equipment and skilled diagnosticians it is frequently impossible to determine whether an erectile problem is psychologically-induced or has an underlying physical basis.

Here, too, previous assumptions about erectile dysfunction are being proved wrong. For instance, it was assumed once that evidence of normal erection in any circumstance – for instance, self-stimultion or morning erection – meant the physical erectile mechanism was fully functional. It is now known that certain blood-flow problems can be relevant in some circumstances but not in others.

Take, for instance, the so-called 'steal syndrome' where erectile failure occurs only once intercourse commences. The man can have a firm erection in a stationary position but, when body movements commence during intercourse, blood is 'stolen' from the penis to the moving muscles in the buttocks. This leads inevitably to anxiety and often to psychologically – induced impotence as well.

Apart from the 'steal syndrome,' blood-flow problems can result in a variety of other symptoms: partial erection where the penile shaft erects but not the glans or vice versa; bowing of the penis due to erection of only one of the two spongy bodies which inflate it; erection without full rigidity; gradual loss of erectile function over months or years.

Various equipment is used to identify the blood-flow problem which may underlie such symptoms. First there's ultrasound equipment, where the reflection of ultrasound waves is used to measure blood flow. Apart from specialist clinics such as the Royal North Shore unit, many urologists in private practice use this equipment.

A new technique developed for the same purpose by Sydney vascular surgeons is infra-red photo-plethysmography. Here, reflection of infra-red radiation is used to pick up arterial flow. The results from this technique appear more accurate and reliable but it is available only at the Royal North Shore unit.

Penile blood pressure measurements give a guide to what's going on inside the penis but if they indicate all is not as it should be, it may be necessary to take a look inside the penis using invasive techniques such as arteriography. This involves the injection of dye into arteries leading to the penis. Computerised serial X-rays are used to follow the movement of the dye through the penile vascular system.

A diagnostic method which is losing favor is nocturnal plethysmography. Here, a small measuring device – a plethysmograph or 'strain gauge' – is attached to the penis. This measures the number of erections and their duration during a night's sleep. Most men have, on average, four erections a night. Unfortunately, nocturnal plethysmography has been found to be influenced by factors which may be irrelevant to normal erectile functioning – fatigue, sleep deprivation, certain types of medication, alcohol and depression. It does not distinguish between tumescence (the ballooning of the penis) and rigidity – a crucial factor if successful intercourse is to occur and one which is affected greatly by vascular problems.

These methods are the main part of the armory for unravelling the vascular component of the diagnostic puzzle. But there is more to an erection than simply blood-flow. A small percentage of erectile problems are contributed to or even caused by neurological conditions and another small percentage by hormonal dysfunction. The latter is the province of the endocrinologist and she or he has hormonal blood tests to apply to the impotent man. Research has indicated that the role of hormones in erectile dysfunction is far less important than was thought.

This is another area where lack of adequate research led to misdiagnosis and therapeutic mismanagement. It all started in the 1960s when hormonal research led to the belief that a deficiency of male hormones could cause erectile failure. It was an attractive theory because it provided an easy solution to impotence – injections of the male hormone testosterone. This fast became the cure-all for all erectile problems. There are thousands of cases of impotent Australian men who have received course after course of testosterone injections to no avail. It has been shown now that the only time testosterone can help is when blood tests show the testicles are not functioning adequately – and this is extremely rare.

There is also a neurological aspect to impotence. Occasionally, it is caused by damage to the nervous system through trauma or accident such as multiple sclerosis or peripheral neuritis (a frequent complication of long-term diabetes). Such neurological causes are as yet untreatable.

Once the problem of correct diagnosis is sorted out, this leaves the question of treatment and here, too, there are developments. In the case of vascular problems, the possibility of surgical treatment depends greatly on the particular vessels affected.

When arterial disease affects large blood vessels, surgery can replace damaged arteries and clean out blockages or widen constricted arteries. Results of surgery on smaller arteries is not so promising. Revascularisation, where grafts from vessels in other parts of the body are used to reconstruct a new blood supply system for the penis, has not yet proved totally successful but research is continuing.

In certain cases of vascular disease, dramatic improvement can result if a heavy smoker is persuaded to give up the habit. There is ample evidence that smoking further constricts arteries damaged by vascular diseases such as arteriosclerosis. Blood flow temperature maps (thermograms) show significant decreases in blood flow to all extremities of the body, including the penis, within seconds of cigarette inhalation.

Many of the vascular problems mentioned are contributed to by other aspects of lifestyle – stress, diet and alcohol are all implicated as well. Of course, such factors also contribute to psychological impotence, so the effect is double-barrelled. Medication for lifestyle-related diseases such as high blood pressure and heart trouble can contribute to erectile dysfunction and sometimes an alternative drug or changes in dosage will rectify the problem. Depression and the medication to treat it also can affect erectile function – an important point often overlooked by sex counsellors.

The complexity of the erectile mechanism means that, once damage is done to the vascular or nervous system, it is difficult to restore normal function. What can be done, however, is to provide an artificial erection.

In the past decade, a variety of models of prostheses has been developed to be inserted surgically into the spongy bodies of the penis. The earliest version was semi-rigid silicon rods which provided a permanent erection. A newer development is a hinged model with a silver central rod, allowing greater flexibility.

Then there is the inflatable prosthesis where the inflation device is controlled by pumps inserted in either testicle.

It is estimated that perhaps 5,000 men worldwide receive penile implants each year, with the United States heading the world in its readiness to adopt this artificial solution.

It is a situation which causes concern to some Australian and European therapists. They argue that there has not been enough long-term assessment of satisfaction with the operation, from the viewpoint of the male and his partner. The evidence is that, while most men are reasonably happy with the results, many are disappointed. Research on partner satisfaction has shown the results often to be less satisfactory from the female point of view.

It is a complex situation, not easy for the therapist attempting to help the impotent man or for the man himself, subject to conflicting opinions from specialists hampered by inadequate research and lacking appropriate diagnostic tools.

A tragedy? Tolstoy thought so: 'Man can endure earthquakes, epidemic, dreadful disease, every form of spiritual torment, but the most dreadful tragedy that can befall him is and will remain the tragedy of the bedroom.'

The Fascination of Sex

What's it Really Like?

'What's it like?' The question was handed in to me on a piece of paper, written by a medical student during a sex question-and-answer session which forms part of their medical course.

What *is* sex like? It stumped me for a moment. Where do you begin to describe the role sex plays in our lives: a source of joy and of misery, a means of comfort and communication, sometimes a weapon, sometimes a giggle, a treat, and for many of us, a subject of endless fascination.

After spending ten years editing and publishing Forum, Australia's first and only serious adult sex education magazine, it was a pleasure to start writing down some of my own ideas about sexuality and relationships. To have the chance to explain to males what women want, what lights our fires and what stifles them. To examine some of the differences between men and women in their sexual attitudes and sexual behaviour, to attempt to promote communication between the sexes and break down some of the barriers to intimacy.

I'm lucky. While I'll never know what it's like to have an erection, or worse, to lose one, I have had the unique experience of hearing firsthand from thousands of men what those and many other personal experiences are like. More and more I have found males eager to talk, to describe what they feel, to ask questions and seek answers to questions about their sexuality.

In recent years I have made deliberate attempts to reach men – writing for a men's magazine, conducting radio talk-back programmes on aspects of male sexuality – and the evidence is that males are now hungry for more information about sex and keen to rid themselves of the burden of having to play the sex expert. Males still feel under pressure to take charge of the action, to pretend to know what they are doing; but secretly, most of them are longing for help in how to please their partners and eager for their turn to lie back and look at the ceiling.

It will come. In recent years there has been a new emphasis on research into male sexuality and we are now discovering all sorts of fascinating information about male sexual response and possibilities for increasing male pleasure. The information is emerging but it's not so easy finding a means of communicating the news to men. Much of what I have written has been published in women's magazines, to be read, we know, not only by females but by boyfriends, husbands, sons and lovers peering over their shoulders. It's not good enough but there's still a battle to persuade traditional media that such matters are worthy of attention in the news magazines, the newspapers, the radio programmes which reach men.

So in the meantime, the sex education continues, tentatively, in the privacy of bedrooms as women gradually learn to teach men what they want, and men slowly learn to listen.

A Revolution in Sex

The sexual revolution. It all sounded so fantastic. They kept telling us it was happening. We were supposed to be living in the midst of a swinging era, a time of sexual change. For most people it was all a bit confusing. It didn't feel like a revolution. *We* certainly weren't changing. Someone else must have been having all the fun.

And now it is apparently all over. In the past ten years the sexual revolution has been and gone. But for everyone who feels they sat on the sidelines reading about it and emerged regretfully untouched, don't kid yourself. This revolution may not have been as much fun as it first sounded, but it did change the bedrooms of our world.

The trouble with living through an era is at the end it's hard to remember what life was like at the beginning. From the standpoint of our present sexual attitudes and behaviour it is hard to imagine the attitudes which existed fifteen years ago. In a book published in 1970, *The Sex Researchers*, Edward Brechner described the change which was then beginning to take place in sexual attitudes.

'We are witnessing a gradual convalescence of our society from a debilitating disease, Victorianism. The essence of the disease is the belief that sex is wicked, loathsome and likely to lead to disaster. Victims of the disease concede that some sex acts are licit – namely coitus from time to time between husband and wife, during the first few decades of marriage, performed in the missionary position, in the dark, for procreation,' Brechner said. Sound strange? Well, fifteen years ago sex did receive a pretty bad press. When sex was discussed publicly it wasn't exactly presented as a normal, healthy activity. The media was fond of horror stories about babies being born 'out of wedlock', VD rates, moral laxity.

We now laugh about Victorians covering up chair legs but in the early 1970s there were still plenty of people around who secretly worried about growing hair on their palms. Sex was a topic which abounded in mythology. Most people knew very little about sex and what they thought they knew was often wrong. It was widely assumed, for instance, that most women had very little interest in sex – and those who did were regarded as nymphomaniacs. Female orgasm had rarely been heard of and the clitoris was quite uncharted territory.

Men were the ones supposed to magically acquire sexual knowledge. The only problem was no one told them where to find it. They were left to fumble around in the dark, pretending they knew what they were doing. While men were afraid to ask women how to make love to them for fear of being seen as inadequate, women were afraid to tell them, and risk bruising the male ego.

Just about ten years ago, for a research project, I advertised in one Sydney newspaper for women who wished to gain more sexual enjoyment. I was swamped by women for whom sex was painful, boring, unenjoyable. There was then ample evidence that sex for most people wasn't all it could be.

I remember talking to a woman who told me about her honeymoon. She had saved herself for the fated night and expected the earth to move, thunderclaps, the works. It was over in two minutes.

She turned to her newly acquired husband and said, 'Is that all there is?'

'I think so,' he said and then after a moment's pause, 'I think I will go and get a hamburger.'

Is that all there is? I'm sure there are plenty of people who are still saying it. But I believe that for most of us the past decade has led to a real increase in our sexual lot. Sex is more pleasurable, more women are reaching orgasm, less are experiencing pain or boredom.

It feels better, we have a better idea of what we are doing. But what about the ratings? Would most people regard their sex lives as more enjoyable than they did ten years ago? I wonder . . . The trouble is that along with giving people the information, the tools they needed to make sex more pleasurable, we also taught them to expect more.

There is no question, that in the promotion of sex there has been a certain amount of overkill. Instead of enjoying and appreciating new-found skills, for some we have created a monster – an endless search for the ultimate elusive orgasm, the dizzy height of ecstasy. That's the trouble with revolutions, they can so easily get out of control.

Before looking more closely at where we are now, it seems sensible to go back to the beginning and see how the whole thing started. What was it that sowed the seeds of this so-called 'revolution'?

Well, in the late 1960s Australia began to see the effects of a number of important events or changes, most of which had originated overseas, particularly in America.

The most dramatic event which was to change the sexual lives of men and women in this country was the development of relatively safe, reliable methods of contraception. For the first time it was possible to isolate procreational sex from sex as recreation; sex for enjoyment free from risk, from worries of unwanted pregnancy. For those of us who grew up with contraception freely available it is hard to imagine the liberating effect the introduction of contraception and accessible medically-safe abortion had on the sexuality of women of previous generations. And now, even with the increasing disillusionment of many women regarding the present contraceptives, there is no way we will return to being the prisoners of biological destiny that our mothers were.

This change coincided with the announcement of the first major sex research. Publication of the work of American researchers Masters and Johnson provided factual information to counter many of the myths about sex which had so many of us barking up quite the wrong tree. Since then we have discovered that some of the conclusions reached by Masters and Johnson were wrong, and no doubt we will have to go on lopping off a few branches until the tree ends up in better shape.

But the impact of this research was immense. First and foremost, it made sex respectable. The fact that sex had been seen as a legitimate area of scientific investigation opened the door to a whole new industry.

The door didn't exactly spring open mind you, it had been shut tight for far too long, but it creaked open over the next few years.

The Masters and Johnson research on the treatment of sexual problems gave a starting point from which to approach an area of therapy which up to then had a fairly dismal track record. Up to this time, a patient with a sexual problem who sought professional advice was either given some seat-of-the-pants counselling (which sometimes made very good sense indeed) or was shoved hastily out the door by the doctor, psychologist or whoever who was embarrassed at being confronted by a problem he or she knew nothing about. The Masters and Johnson work gave us all a starting point and since then their techniques have been refined, and in some cases discarded.

Without doubt, some of the credit for setting the ball rolling in the 1960s and early 1970s must go to the media. The discoveries in sex research and therapy were, of course, a gift horse to the media and journalists had no intention of looking it in the mouth.

The same new-found respectability that was helping doctors to stop shying away from the subject, enabled the media to discuss in detail topics they wouldn't have dared mention only a few years before.

In the early 1970s there were endless newspaper articles, discussions on radio and television analysing the new sex research and its implications. We saw the launching of new women's magazines, which published comprehensive informative articles on sexuality, female sexual anatomy, physiology, orgasm, sexual technique. These magazines, along with specialist publications such as *Forum*, educated a generation of Australian women.

For the first time women were being taught about their own sexuality and encouraged to take a more active role in sex, no more lying back and thinking of England, no more leaving it all up to the male. They were given information about their bodies, about their genitals. They were taught about sexual arousal, orgasm, sexual technique. They learnt to expect sex to be an enjoyable experience in which they were to play an equal role.

Of couse this concept of equality in sex tied in very nicely with another important influence during this time – the women's movement. Sex was a great cause for women. It was an area in which women generally had been having a pretty rough deal, the vast majority apparently didn't enjoy it very much yet felt obliged to participate to fulfill their marital duties. The basic message was right but unfortunately the way it was presented did us all a hell of a disservice.

The problem was many of the first writers in the women's movement were inclined to see women's lack of enjoyment as totally the fault of men. Men didn't know what women wanted, they were purely after their own pleasure, they made assumptions about female sexuality, deprived us of our sexual rights. Why, they even hid our clitorises from us by writing anatomy books which omitted any mention of this delicate little organ.

Strong stuff . . . and it left Australian men reeling under a blow from which they have not yet recovered. Men knew their wives were reading innumerable articles entitled 'Is your husband a lousy lover?' Often they knew or suspected their women didn't enjoy sex much . . . but they didn't know what to do about it. They couldn't talk to anyone about it . . . just as real men don't eat quiche, real men certainly don't lean against the bar and tell their mates about their fears that their wives aren't enjoying sex or their worries about not getting it up. Therapists, doctors are still finding it so much easier for women than men to seek advice about a sexual problem or ask for sexual information. Men are still brought up to hide their emotions, keep their feelings to themselves. They have also been taught to regard sex as an area in which they have to compete with other men, to score, to perform. With this sort of upbringing it's not surprising males are very vulnerable to attacks on their sexual performance. By attacking them, by criticising their performance, women have simply made it harder for men to learn to change. The whole situation is rather like forcing the blind man to lead the guide dog and kicking him when he can't find his way home.

So this is probably the most important message to emerge from the past decade of study and discussion of sexuality. If women wish to enjoy sex more, they must take responsibility for their own arousal. If we approach female satisfaction in this way and make the woman's pleasure her own responsibility, it takes an enormous load off the male. He doesn't have to fumble around wondering if he is doing the right thing. The essence of this approach is that it removes female response from the domain of the male ego. Actually, keeping ego out of sex is a major preoccupation with therapists these days and is a sad indication of one of the areas in which the sexual revolution has created new problems. There is no doubt that for many people, both men and women, sex has become a competition in which they feel under pressure to perform. There is a real element of 'keeping up with the Joneses' as people constantly compare their sexual lives with what they read about.

Sex becomes overly important, when it *doesn't* work. If a couple are experiencing problems with relating sexually, sex can very easily become an obsession which, if left untreated, can poison an otherwise perfectly good relationship.

Looking at the effect this type of pattern can have on loving relationships makes me very glad that we are now so much better equipped to deal with sexual problems. It has been tremendously exciting to be involved in sex therapy in the past decade. Our knowledge of the causes of sexual problems has increased dramatically; theories which were being expounded only five or ten years ago have been completely overturned.

A classic example of an area in which sexologists have had to eat their words is impotence: the inability of a male to gain or maintain an erection. Ten years ago it was thought that 90–95 per cent of impotency was due to purely psychological causes, it was all in the mind. The bad news in recent research suggests that up to 40 to 50 per cent of impotency has a physical cause. The list of possible contributing factors is huge: diabetes, nervous system disorders, thyroid disease, some forms of pituitary disease, severe depression, arteriosclerosis, drugs including alcohol plus some medication for high blood pressure and depression.

What is really depressing from the therapists' point of view is that once many of these physical problems exist, there is not all that much we can do about them. The mechanism which controls erection is extremely delicate, and although drug therapy or surgery may produce some solutions, for many males, once they have allowed their health to affect their sexual functioning, they can't expect to ever regain their former prowess. The lesson here for women is that if we want men who can continue to gain strong erections through their lives – and there are plenty of males who can do this – we had better teach them to look after their health. I suspect if an anti-smoking, anti-drinking campaign were to concentrate on the effects these drugs have on male sexual performance, it may have more effect than present attempts to confront people with their own mortality.

Of course from the female point of view, this emphasis on erections may not be all that important. One of the other major discoveries in the past decade was the fact that most women find it difficult to climax during intercourse purely through vagina-penis contact and require additional direct stimulation of the clitoris. For most of these women they are far more likely to climax through oral stimulation or by manual stimulation of the clitoris than through intercourse. The emphasis in our culture on intercourse as *the real thing*, the ultimate form of lovemaking means many women miss out on the stimulation which is most likely to give them maximum physical pleasure (although many enjoy the closeness and emotional satisfaction of coitus). Since we made this discovery, it has been possible to help many women to change their concept of what is normal. They no longer need to worry about being different or frigid and can enjoy their orgasms, however they are caused.

In the meantime there have also been some important new discoveries which may assist those women who would still like to increase their vaginal sensitivity. Even the much maligned G spot (yes, it does exist, but apparently not in *all* women!) has a role to play here – it's not the golden fleece, but simply an area worth exploring as one possible source of sexual enjoyment.

These discoveries are enlarging the pool of knowledge about sexuality which will help men and women in the future understand and enjoy their sexuality more fully. When you think back to how little we knew about sex ten or fifteen years ago and how much of what we thought we knew turned out to be a mish-mash of misconceptions, half-truths, twisted by moral beliefs, 'revolution' doesn't seem too strong a word to describe the change which has occurred.

I believe it has been a change for the better, despite some casualties. Now that we have all calmed down somewhat and sex isn't the bestseller it used to be, the turmoil of a revolution may give way to slower progress towards a mature understanding of one of the great joys of life.

Sexual Worlds Apart

Man and woman. Two different sexual worlds and a huge gulf between us. Oh sure, there are exceptions. There *are* males who crave intimacy as a prelude to every sexual encounter. There *are* women who can use sex to escape from the tensions of the day, but for most of us there is a distinctive male and female approach to sex and no matter how hard we try, the twain never seem to meet. After years of talking to men and women about their sexual needs, it seems to me that some of the differences are irreconcilable. In some crucial ways the sexual needs of women are different from the sexual needs of men, and even with the best will in the world, we'll never quite understand what it's like on the other side of the fence.

'Talk, talk talk! He tries to convince me; I try to convince him. What's the use? It's not the words that are missing. I don't even know if the problem is that we don't understand each other. We understand, all right. But we don't like what we know; that's the problem.' As a married woman in her mid-thirties points out, we can talk about male and female needs and desires, think about them, read about them, but however strenuous and honest our attempt at communication between the sexes, the gap still exists. Chalk and cheese.

Think I'm being unduly pessimistic? I know it is now fashion-able to think of men and women as basically the same ilk – these days we are all supposed to be androgynous under the skin and with the right sort of encouragement both the male and female sides of our characters can flourish and bloom.

But when it comes to sex, there seems a limit to how much our roles can merge. I'm not talking about the old 'Me Tarzan, You Jane' routine. Everyone seems pretty happy nowadays to do away with the passive female, active male charade. As a female it is wonderful to be able to throw in a few helpful hints here and there and force him to lie back while you torment him for a change. Most men are happy to let go the reins occasionally and let them-selves be led. Actually, I think it's during the initial throes of passion that men and women are often most similar, displaying a similar degree of lust and mutual delight at discovering the joys of sex together.

It's in the long haul that the sexual gender differences really emerge. When you have been living together or married a year or so and both come home hassled and tense after a hard day's work, it shows. All a woman wants to do is put her feet up, and let the tension drain out of her while describing in gory detail the horrors of her day – accompanied, of course, by an occasional sympathetic grunt or a 'there-there' or two from him and a sooth-ing pat on the arm or neck massage. Sex is the last thing on her mind. But as for him, well, men seem to have this extraordinary capacity to use sex as an escape. Sex for them, for many of them, can be the means to a relaxed end. For us females, or at least for me and most of my friends, it works the other way.

How many women do you know who are interested in sex when they are really exhausted? You've just shifted house, lugging box after box of household goods up and down flights of stairs. You eat cold baked beans out of the tin standing up in the kitchen and then collapse together into bed. You're just drifting off and then you feel it. You look over at him. He's really half-asleep, worn out, but there's his eager member till keen to round off the day. Men live in a different sexual world, a private fantasy-filled love-life that is their escape from the bustle of everyday life. I've often envied them their ability to tune out and be carried off by the power of the fantasies and pleasure of their bodies.

Wouldn't it be wonderful if we could do that too? Instead we lie there worrying about whether we remembered to buy more muesli for breakfast and what on earth is Johnny going to wear in the school play. We are simply not good at concentrating on what we are supposed to be doing. Why can't we forget that his mother is in the next room or our teenage son is still out in the car? Why must we keep one ear alert in case the baby wakes up? Why can't *we* use sex to escape?

Melbourne writer and sociologist Beatrice Faust wrote a fascinating book on differences in the sexual styles of men and women. The book, published by Penguin (1980) under the title *Women, Sex & Pornography*, gathered evidence demonstrating the differences between the sexes, finally reaching the depressing conclusion that 'much of the time men and women do not seem to be complementary or even compatible'.

Faust discusses the research showing females are more sensitive to touch. Baby girls have been found to have a lower pain threshold than males and develop greater sensitivity more rapidly than baby boys. Female babies are more sensitive to the removal of coverings and to exposure to a jet of air. Males are more visual than tactile. They are more readily aroused by visual stimuli, responding more readily to erotica, pornography and are more easily aroused by observing the opposite sex. Male sexuality is more easily conditioned than female sexuality. It is rare for a woman to acquire a sexual fetish where her sexual interest is directed towards objects rather than her sexual partner. Yet most men are somewhat aroused by the trappings of sex – sexy underwear, suspenders, long boots. It is predominantly males who develop the weird and wonderful sexual preferences, the uncommon sexual practices which usually show a history of sexual conditioning.

The result is that men go to bed with their imaginations. Their sexual appetites are stimulated and sustained by a whole range of erotic images and events which have gone before or are likely to happen in the future. Kinsey was one of the first to point this out; 'As far as his psychologic responses are concerned, the male in many instances may not be having coitus with the immediate sexual partner, but with all of the other girls with whom he has ever had coitus, and with the entire genus Female with which he would like to have coitus.'

In his book, *The Sexual Behaviour Of The Human Male* (W.B. Saunders, New York, 1948), Kinsey talked about the differences in male and female sexual drive which result from the male's ability to be conditioned by his sexual environment. Kinsey felt the male goes through life picking up and responding to all sorts of visual erotic cues which feed his sexual imagination. He then parcels these up and takes them to bed with him . . . Hey presto, an instant source of arousal which exists totally independently of the rest of his world and of his relationships.

It makes men very versatile. They may well prefer intimacy but they don't need it in the same way as women do. They *can* settle for raw sex, with no side dishes. Remember that peculiarly male joke about not needing to look at the mantelpiece while stoking the fire? Well, many men are able to respond in extraordinary and trying circumstances, with women they find unsympathetic or unattractive. They can use their imaginations to light their fires and keep them sexually on heat.

We are different. Instead of being able to be swept away by flights of fantasy, we get bogged down in the here and now. In a wonderfully sensitive book called *Gender – The Myth Of Equality*, American surgeon James C. Neely talks about the female's inability to stand outside herself. 'Men and women react differently in their sex to the events of the day, indicating again how sex to a woman is more a totality of existence, to man it is or can be something apart. Measurements of men's depressions, periods of boredom, episodes of success and failure, or introversion have little or no influence on the frequency of heterosexual performance. What such mood dispositions do seem to influence is indulgence in erotic fantasy and self-arousal, both of which markedly decreased when man is moody. But sex is little affected. 'This is not the case with woman whose working day gives her cause to feel sexy or not sexy. Sexually speaking she cannot stand outside herself and still enjoy sex as a man can at the end of a bad day. Which does not mean that she can't or won't partici- pate. But she is not apt to enjoy herself for herself, as he is himself, under such trying circumstances. Women have always marvelled at how men can perform "even when they don't feel good".'

Nowhere is the difference between the sexes so clearly demon- strated than in male and female homosexuality. Lesbian couples generally show little interest in casual sex. They tend to form inti- mate emotional relationships where sex is rarely centre stage. Although there are homosexual males who form similar commit- ted monogamous relationships, gay males are notorious for their interest in impersonal, anonymous, casual sex. The public bath- houses and steambaths provide gays with a steady diet of high- sensation, low-emotion sex. Put males together and you see mas- culine sexual behaviour at its most blatant.

Beatrice Faust wonders if the characteristics which predominate in female sexuality – our enjoyment of touching, need for inti- macy, our emphasis on here-and-now pleasure – are designed to fit us for motherhood. It is an unfashionable biology-is-destiny argument but very convincing when you think about the impor- tance of sensitivity and touching in caring for babies and the intimacy that is the essence of the nurturant mother-child rela- tionship. Research has shown that mothers have unique hearing: they can pick their baby's cry from among dozens of others. Perhaps our sexual distractibility is a biologically-based protec- tive mechanism to care for the young. Someone has to be there ready for a plaintive cry. Someone needs to keep their feet on the ground rather than trip off all the time to erotic dream worlds.

As a mother, it's an explanation which makes sense to me. It does seem that the period when we are bogged down in child- rearing is the time when male-female differences in sexual drive cause the most stress and strain on our relationships. Perhaps motherhood is supposed to drive away our lovers, temporarily at least, until the birds have left the nest.

And then afterwards perhaps, we're ready to move towards sexual androgyny. Talking to men and women about these ideas, it's surprising how many older women comment that their sexuality has changed over time, their needs have become more 'male'. Many women seem gradually to learn to tune out as men do, to indulge in fantasies, to be less easily distracted. Many women experience a sexual burst of energy in their late thirties, forties or even later when they find themselves seeking sexual variety, needing intimacy less and raw sex more. And do males become more female in their sexual needs? I'm not sure – certainly older men are more inclined to talk to me about enjoying touching and sensuality, and enjoying intimacy as part of their sexual relationships. I've always thought it's just that men grow up sexually. How's that for female chauvinism? Perhaps they just grow more female! It's a nice theory and a nice thought as we age, we may better learn to understand each other's sexual needs and share the same desires. Yet I'm sure it's not so easy. In many of us, our sexual patterns become entrenched and our differences simply provide fuel for a very sad battle between the sexes.

At this point let me repeat what I said in the beginning: I know there *are* exceptions to these patterns. I *am* making sweeping generalisations and there are many men and women who feel differently and behave differently. As we all know, there is an enormous amount of individual difference between women in their sexual needs and desires and between men. All these ideas are based on an overall view of male and female sexuality and even now, the differences between the sexes may be changing.

There is no doubt that since many of the sexual taboos have been lifted, *some* of the differences between the sexes in attitudes and behaviour have disappeared. As women learn to discover and enjoy their sexuality earlier in their lives as a result of the sex education they now receive at schools, from their community and the women's magazines such as *Dolly* and *Cleo*, it may be that female desire will be less affected by the hassles of daily life.

Already all sorts of assumed differences between the sexes have been disproved or at least diluted. Although it is true that most women seem less aroused by visual stimulation than men, more women now feel comfortable about acknowledging they enjoy looking at nude male bodies, enjoy and are aroused by some forms of pornography, and are happy to indulge in that traditionally male pursuit, voyeurism – or in this case, crutch watching. Often the sexual differences which did exist between the sexes were culturally imposed. Women had fewer affairs than males, indulged less frequently in pre-marital sex, and exhibited less interest in unusual sexual practices, not because this is the way they are but because this was the way they were expected to behave.

Now, in all these areas, women are showing more interest and indulging more freely in such pursuits. In fact, occasionally, much to the male's surprise, it is the female who turns out to have the most voracious appetite. Take for example, swinging. Group sex or partner swapping has for a long time been predominantly a male fantasy. Research shows it is usually the male who persuades his reluctant wife to enter the group scene, yet it is often the female who thrives on it. The evidence is that many females take to swinging like a duck to water, and it is the males who subsequently become concerned to find their wives revelling in the new-found sexual variety.

So it may well be that some of the present gulf between the sexes will ultimately disappear. But there is one area of conflict which is particularly intransigent, probably the major source of sexual strife between couples – the relationship between sex and intimacy.

Intimate Strangers by American psychologist Lillian B. Rubin (Harper & Row, New York, 1983) looks at the conflicts that occur between men and women as a result of their differing needs for intimacy. Drawing on detailed interviews and discussions with over 200 couples, the book contains some telling quotes from both husbands and wives about their differing sexual needs. Lillian Rubin shows that even if men and women make efforts to communicate, it doesn't make the sexual issues any less intransigent.

When women seek the intimacy they need to feel ready for sex, they often require some concrete gesture, some demonstration of thought and feeling, as shown by these comments from two of Rubin's subjects; 'I want to know what he's thinking, you know, what's going on inside him – before we jump into bed' (woman); and 'To me, there's a nice bond when we're together – just reading the paper or watching the tube, or something. Then, when we go to bed that's not enough for her' (man).

Doesn't that ring true. 'What are you thinking?' she says. 'Nothing' he replies. As females we poke and probe trying to find out what's happening inside the inner world of our men. The trouble is often men don't know what they are feeling.

In interviewing men, Lillian Rubin found it was a common experience to ask a man, 'How does that feel?' and see a blank look come over his face. Females need words, use words to describe feelings and share experiences with other women.

'For the woman, intimacy without words is small comfort most of the time,' Lillian Rubin says. 'It's not that she needs always to talk, but it's important to her to know what's going on inside him if she's to feel close. And it's important for her to believe he cares what's going on inside her.'

And for men, their intimacy may not need talk or gestures. Often for them, intimacy comes with sex. Sex is the one place they can let their emotions out, even wallow in them, and not feel unmanly. As one said, 'Having sex with her makes me feel much closer, so it makes it easier to bridge the emotional gap, so to speak. It's as though the physical sex opens up another door, and things and feelings can get expressed that I couldn't bring out before.'

Perhaps, in the end, that's what makes sex so special. When sex is good and you lie there with arms around you, finally the barriers between you can come down. You can share his inner world. In that brief vulnerable moment, that's the time when men and women are most alike; when the things that separate are blown away. Those precious moments of closeness can even make the rest of the battles seem worthwhile.

Giving Sex a Bad Name . . .

'Get off the table Mabel, the money's for the beer.' It's an old pub ditty supposed to represent the Australian male's attitude to sex.

Looking at what's happening to men and women in bed today, it wouldn't surprise me at all if more and more males chose to stick to their beer. Sex is fast become a battlefield, with women calling most of the shots. What really worries me is that if women keep on the way they are, the enemy will stage a retreat, licking their wounds.

And then we will have no one to play with. That's the real point. Sex was designed to be fun, a gentle romp. Not a competition. Not a means of scoring points, of fighting battles for liberation. I'd be the first to agree that for a long time sex was weighted in the male's favour. Men did have all the fun while females were left high and dry – 'dry' being the operative word. Ouch! But even then the fault was as much with women as with men. With mothers who taught their daughters to expect sex to be boring and painful and with daughters who believed them and never gave it a chance to be different. That's all past history and if we persist in trying to use sex to right these wrongs, we all stand to lose. Obviously men today have inherited many of the attributes which previously gave women a hard time in bed, but if we desire them to change, to be the considerate, sensitive lovers we claim to want, we must lead the way.

'A hard time in bed' is a telling phrase. Whether we like it or not, men are extremely vulnerable. They have been brought up to regard sex as a test of their manhood, erections as proof of their masculinity. Fine, many of us may not want erections, we may not need intercourse for our sexual satisfaction. But we still want our males to show they find us attractive, to let us know they are having a good time. The penis is a great barometer of a man's sexual condition and there's every indication just at the moment that he's experiencing some extremely stormy weather.

The other day I was listening to a friend, an attractive liberated woman, complaining that she never meets any men who are decent lovers. She is always bedding men who don't seem to know the first thing about how to satisfy her and who take it as an insult when she throws in a few suggestions. And what's more, they don't even seem to enjoy it.

And listen to Catherine: 'I've just about given up on relationships. I'm discouraged. I've seen so many men in the past year. More than half of them couldn't get or keep it up. Those that could, couldn't care less about pleasing me. The big effort was usually: can they keep their erections? What's wrong with men these days with their erections? I'd give anything to meet a decent, nice man who enjoyed sex, could get erections, and cared about pleasing me too.'

What's wrong with men? I think both of these women, if they sat down and thought about it, would know what's wrong with the men they go to bed with. As one woman admitted to her husband: 'I guess if I were a man I could count on getting erections maybe 30 per cent of the time.'

In what has become the politics of potency, we're less interested in erections, in male orgasms as by-products of their pleasure than as proof of our own desirability. These women, many women, are depending on dutiful erections because underneath it all they are worried that the demand for sexual satisfaction is threatening to men. It's a real double bind. They want to be able to ask for what *they* want. They want males to be able to satisfy them but they are also insisting males enjoy it, *all the time.*

That's where the system breaks down and that's where Catherine and my friend would realise they are being unrealistic if they thought carefully about it. As women we all know that during the process of learning to make love to someone there are times when our focus on learning how to give pleasure means a drop in our own arousal. When you are sorting out the messages, tuning into his response, your own arousal is distracted. Our own fluctuations in the arousal are far less obvious than the male's, whose penis waxes and wanes as he concentrates on pleasing us in between letting himself just flow with his own pleasure. We can't have our cake and eat it too. When men take time to learn about us, we can't expect the penis to stand constantly to attention.

The problem with men and erections is partly in their heads but partly in ours. We don't *need* a constant erection to enjoy ourselves (and neither does he). In fact, fluctuations in firmness can provide an opportunity to experiment with different sensations, different feelings.

It takes time to learn these things and none of us is immune. The breakthrough for me personally came through a relationship with a man who took for granted the natural ebb and flow of his erections as he tuned in and out of his experience and mine. His comfort, his complete naturalness made me realise how much in the past I joined in precisely the type of 'results-watching' I had always criticised in males. I had taken my ego to bed with me and the minute I encountered any deviation from the old ever-ready, panting-at-the-leash version of male sexuality, I started wondering what was wrong with me.

I remember once, in a previous relationship, wondering if the man I was with had reached orgasm. I was immediately swamped by a wave of anxiety. I found myself thinking all these crazy thoughts that had more to do with my own ego than what was happening to him. Was I too wet? Was I less of a 'snug fit' after having my baby? I vowed to be more diligent about my vaginal exercises . . . I needed his orgasm as proof of my attractiveness and desirability. And I didn't even *know* for sure whether or not he had had one. If he hadn't, did he *want* to and was there something he wanted me to do about it? But was I putting pressure on him if I did ask if he had?

To ask or not to ask? Here's where the new rules of sexual etiquette become very difficult indeed, particularly for the man. He really can't win. He knows he shouldn't pretend to know what to do, these days he's allowed to *ask* to be pointed in the right directions. So she throws him a few hints which he tries to interpret and put into action. She's trying not to play the traffic cop – left, right, do this, do that – so her instructions tend to be rather vague. He is expected to show interest in her arousal but not exert pressure, to persevere with his attempts to please her without making her feel he expects results.

But at the end of it all, how does he know when and if he's allowed to stop? Endless books, various articles in women's magazines have sneered at the insensitive oaf who dares to voice that vulgar refrain: 'Didja come?' How does a sensitive, concerned man find out if a woman is being satisfied without his question being seen as an expectation or demand? How does he avoid looking as if he's trying to find out how well he did?

Men I talk to are well aware of the hazards of this emotional minefield. Listen to them:

'Usually I ask – even though I have a picture in my mind of an obnoxious clod who finishes having sex with a woman (coming as fast as possible) and then asks: "Didja come?"'

'I no longer ask, as my questions were taken as accusations – as they were once intended.'

'I used to ask because I wasn't sure. I'm sorry now that I did because it was embarrassing for her. I also know she was faking it and lying about it.'

'If I am in doubt I do ask. Some women get upset and shy and say, "Couldn't you tell?" So sometimes I won't say anything and let her voluntarily say whether she did or didn't. Depending on the woman, it can be a touchy situation.'

'The only thing that really irritates me about women is their resentment over being asked whether or not they have had, or are ready to have an orgasm. When a man is concerned about this, it does not mean that he is nagging or imposing some sort of responsibility; it means, rather, that he *is* being considerate. And the women who imagine that the soft contractions of a moist, dilated vagina can be sensed by a penis urgently striving to release semen, while its owner is straining to hold the fluid in and stay rigid, are imagining one helluva lot.'

Is it any wonder some of them feel like giving up, seeking solace in their beer? It doesn't exactly sound all that much like fun, does it? We mustn't forget just how far men have come in such a short time. I remember sometime ago hearing Shere Hite complaining that for years women have been serving men orgasms like coffee: 'Now women are saying "My coffee days are over".'

Well, I still like serving coffee . . . to the right man. So much of the real joy of sex is giving pleasure, the gentle art of learning how to please. I'm sure that in the past many women enjoyed ladling out those endless cups of coffee. Men didn't have to worry about delaying ejaculation, about female orgasms. I suspect most of them had a pretty good time and their women enjoyed giving them a good time. And whether we like to or not, even then plenty of women had their own orgasms along the way. Now the rules have changed but in our eagerness to achieve sexual equality for women, are we destroying the essence of sexual give-and-take? Instead of revelling in our partner's pleasure, we seem constantly to be checking a balance sheet to make sure he doesn't draw ahead.

Okay, we know it isn't necessary for women to climax in inter-course. But does this mean we have to sneer at men who still enjoy this form of lovemaking? I hear so many women complain about having to put up with intercourse just to please their lovers. For example: 'I was totally passive. I used to fake orgasms to keep men happy. I was really a sex object. When I got into feminism, I stopped faking orgasms and started to insist on not having penetration if I didn't want it. I found I didn't want it that much and I got rid of men who couldn't cope.'

Men and women don't *have* to enjoy the same things at the same time. It's nice to take turns, to do something he enjoys and get high on his pleasure before you taste your own special treat. When sex really works, your response is his aphrodisiac, his pleasure your greatest reward. But I don't want to imply it's all so easy. So often a request seems like a demand. An attempt to please becomes a performance. We all tend to play to the gallery, unable to forget tomorrow's reviews.

It's a slow process but I'm learning. I can now reach for a man's hand and show him what I want. I can tell him to keep doing something that feels terrific. I'm not nearly as good at finding the words to tell him to stop doing something that doesn't. I'm trying to avoid pressuring men into dutiful erections, learning not to assume he will *always* be interested. Some time ago I found myself launching into a complicated explanation as to why I didn't want to go to bed with a very attractive man I'd met. For me, it was a case of wrong place, wrong time but plenty of regrets. How foolish I felt when he said with a sigh of relief that he'd felt just the same and really preferred a cuddle. How arrogant, how typically female had been my assumption that he'd wanted to.

One of the reasons men find it so hard to rid themselves of traditional male approaches to sex is we females constantly confuse them by expecting them to behave as cave-men and being disappointed when they aren't dragging us off by the hair. We ask men to empathise with us, to understand our feelings, be aware of our vulnerabilities. But are we willing to allow them the same freedom? Are we ready to accept *he* may not always feel like having sex or getting an erection or having an orgasm?

If we really want a man with gentle hands, a tender touch, that's the price we'll have to pay. But it's worth it. There is much to be gained from throwing away the myths, the gameplaying and learning to make friends with our lovers.

Blat Sex

One day a teenage boy asked his father if women feel different sensations during sex than men. 'Oh, yes,' the father said, 'for women it's like a symphony, building from a quiet song to a rich, melodious rhythm that bursts into a magnificent crescendo, repeating itself in waves of music that gradually fade to a quiet denouement.' 'And for men?' asked the boy. 'Well, it's like one high note on a trumpet,' said his father, 'BLAT.'

It's a joke, or is it? Like most of the stories swapped over bar tables about sex, it contains more than its fair share of truth. Female sexuality, female arousal, has always been regarded as a complex, mysterious process. The male lover is encouraged to be the artisan, the creative master who draws out the woman's sensuous response, who plays her body like an instrument so that she is swept by mysterious erotic forces to her inevitable, earth shaking climax. The poets, the writers, they speak in flowing language of female arousal, the flame of desire to be coaxed into light, the waves of passion, the gentle undulations of her body as her pleasure builds up. She is the symphony, the waves of the ocean, the flowers bursting into blossom. And he. He is the achiever, the doer. No symphonies for him. In all the erotic novels he's simply the one who makes it happen. You never hear of his waves, his symphonies, he plays her instrument, not his own.

Does that add up to blat sex? I suspect it does. My experience from years of talking to males about their sexuality is that very few men ever have the chance to explore their real sexual potential. For many, their pleasure comes from playing the instrument, from enjoying giving the woman pleasure. To achieve this goal they learn to control their own sexuality, to hold back, block out their own sensations.

Of course, these are the good lovers, the sensitive souls who realise lovemaking involves more than the traditional wham-bam-thank-you-m'am. And there are still plenty of men who treat sex like a 100-metre dash with their own orgasm as the only prize. But for the ones who are trying to make lovemaking something more than that, it may well be that despite the pleasure of conducting her symphony, his own sexuality ends up a rather blat affair.

This came home to me when talking to a friend of mine, Julia, a very sexual women in her mid-thirties who has had experience with a range of lovers. She's aware of the pleasure her response gives them. 'Most of my partners have been amazed at how responsive I am and get a great thrill from playing with me and seeing just how high they can get me. I'm lucky enough to be able to have numerous orgasms, continuous orgasms for long periods of time and most guys really do enjoy counting how many I have and all that stuff. It's part of that whole male competitive thing – I don't mind really, but sometimes I find it sad that I'm the one who is up there floating around in the clouds and all they can do is cheer from the sidelines. They are just not into their own pleasure.'

Julia became aware of just how rare it is for a male to be pleasure oriented when she had an affair with a man who was just as keen to reach dizzy heights of ecstasy as she was; 'It was an amazing sexual relationship. Right from the beginning I was aware that there was something different about Dave. He wasn't particularly interested in my orgasms and certainly never counted them – he just couldn't have done any counting because he was just as far off the planet as I was. I was so aware of his pleasure. Like me, he would play with his sensations, allow them to build up and up and then let them subside, teasing himself with how far he would let himself go. 'I was surprised to find he was able to have multiple orgasms without ejaculation, but he said he had just learned to enjoy orgasmic sensations through playing around with his response. It was amazing for me to be with him because I learnt to *feel* where he was – we were so tuned in to each other that we could both let our orgasms trigger each other off. It was so different being with a man who was having as much fun as I was – or perhaps even more!'

The experience with Dave has convinced Julia that most men do miss out on an enormous amount of pleasure; 'Since Dave, I have found it really strange being with men who seem so tuned out to what's happening in their bodies. It's flattering and sweet that they do appreciate my pleasure, but it's still not the same as being with someone who's sharing the same highs. I'm lucky that I do respond so easily so I'm not put off by the male watching me to see what a good job he's doing as a lover. But for other women who have difficulty climaxing . . . friends of mine constantly complain that guys pressure them into feeling they have to have orgasms to make the male feel successful. Perhaps if the guys focussed more on their own enjoyment, it would reduce that type of pressure.'

It is certainly true that male desire to give a woman pleasure can well become a two-edged sword when she feels under pressure to respond for the sake of his ego. A woman wrote to me, recently, complaining of her difficulty in responding in front of her husband; 'I have been married for sixteen years and my husband has told me there is nothing he wouldn't do for me sexually. He tries very hard, or maybe too hard, to turn me on. I enjoy sex once I'm involved, but it's hard to reach that feeling. I feel very uneasy about myself and my actions. It's hard to let myself go completely because I feel as if I'm on show in front of him. To me his eyes always seem to be popping out waiting for something to happen.'

So many of us have our watcher in the shadows, the eager man who seeks proof that his endeavours to please have borne fruit – namely our orgasms. It's an unfortunate consequence of the role men are expected to play in sex. For as long as men (and women) see the male as the person in charge of the sexual action, the initiator, the person who makes it all happen, it is inevitable that the male ego will be dragged into the action. Many men do see female sexual response as proof of their masculine success – so much so that sex becomes a performance, a test of their skill, and their own enjoyment is neglected in their attempts to live up to the masculine ideal.

Perhaps one way of reducing these pressures would be to help men focus more attention on their own pleasure. If men could be taught to see their own sexual response as something other than a battle to keep control while the woman indulges herself, they may become less interested in producing female orgasms or counting how many they have. They may learn to enjoy the pleasurable sensations of early arousal, to revel in the rise and fall of waves of pleasure, to create their own symphony. They may even find that orgasm isn't quite as important as they thought – and in the process may learn to understand us females that much better.

Well what is it that stops men from discovering these things naturally? Why do they need to be taught? Part of the answer lies in the fact that males do focus so much attention on learning to do things for the woman. As one young man pointed out to me: 'When you are with a partner you are intent on making your partner feel good – doing wonders for her. It's part of the ego thing. It makes you feel good to deliver. You want to stay in control so that means you tend to shy away when it does feel good because you're afraid that you'll blow it. So you hold back and don't let yourself think too much about what's happening to you.'

He was a young guy who was very conscious of the problem of coming too quickly. He learnt to avoid thinking about what was happening to him for fear that this would take him over the top. Yet when I talked to him about whether he had ever experimented with how long he could enjoy the pleasurable sensations of build up of arousal, he said he simply never let himself think about that while making love. His focus was on keeping control, blocking out sensation rather than experimenting with his own pleasure and learning to spin that out. 'I suppose you subconsciously hold back and really don't think you can afford to explore pleasure too much – there's always the danger of going too far.'

It seems a common pattern – the young man whose sex energy is devoted to blocking sensation, holding back for fear of coming too quickly, and then after a while it just becomes a pattern to stay tuned out – focussing just on what's happening to her. Many males deliberately learn to think of non-sexual, even gloomy, depressing or frightening things during sex to stop themselves ejaculating – it's no wonder they can hardly manage a trumpet blast after dampeners like that.

Dr Bob Montgomery, a Melbourne clinical psychologist and author, is well known through his television and radio appearances giving advice on sex and relationship problems. Dr Montgomery feels that the male's early sexual experiences teach him to set low goals for his own sexual pleasure; 'Most males are conditioned early into being rather selfish about sex. Their illicit early masturbating experiences have taught them to get it over with as quickly as possible. They take these habits with them into their first sexual experiences – sex becomes a quick screw followed by ejaculation. These experiences mislead the guys into setting low goals for themselves and it is easy for them to think that's what sex is all about. 'Then later they may become more sophisticated and learn they have to become concerned about their partner's sexual response, but as they raise their sights to put more effort into their partner's enjoyment, they often allow their own sexual pleasure to fall behind.'

Dr Montgomery says many males do become expert at suppressing their own response; 'It's part of the whole masculinity stake. He becomes terribly concerned about what she will think of him and not sufficiently concerned about himself. His ego becomes more important than his pleasure. Since he's expected to play the expert role, not just in sex, he's reluctant to ask for help, he's reluctant to experiment with his own enjoyment for fear of not performing well enough. To have the courage to explore his own pleasure, a guy has to feel safe enough within his relationship to break the rules, and to let her take charge.'

In fact, one of the benefits of men learning to be more aware of the ebb and flow of their sexual arousal patterns is that by tuning into the pleasure, they are able to extend the period they can last without ejaculating. Men who become attuned to the subtle changes that occur during their arousal cycle, and particularly the changes that occur during the period just before ejaculation, usually develop their own techniques for preventing ejaculation, techniques based on all sorts of physical tricks from briefly stopping movement, to squeezing muscles in the pelvic area, deep breathing or whatever. The key is self-awareness and experimentation to find out what works best for them.

But it's not just concern about ejaculation control that stops men exploring their sexual potential; part of the problem seems simply a lack of awareness that it is possible for men to experience something different. Just as twenty years ago there were many women who never realised it was possible for women to experience orgasm, there are now many men who are unaware that they can experience more than blat sex.

I have talked on radio and written numerous articles about some of the new discoveries about male sexuality . . . the fact that men can learn to have multiple orgasms, and orgasms with ejaculation, the differences between a true orgasmic experience and simple ejaculation, techniques for increasing male pleasure. Wherever I go, I now encounter men who say they were surprised to hear that such things were possible for them.

Well, they are possibilities, and may even things up a little – provided we don't take all these tricks and techniques too seriously. For despite all this emphasis on physical pleasure, sexual techniques form only a tiny part of the give and take that contributes to a good relationship. If the balance is there it's a start – men and women having equal opportunities to discover and enjoy their sexual potential.

Man and His Penis

He can't sleep. He nudges his dozing partner. 'Just once more,' he pleads softly. 'I'll be gentle, I *promise*.'

His mate responds with something less than wild enthusiasm. 'Leave me alone. This is the third time in about an hour and a half! Don't you ever think about anything else?'

In case you are wondering what woman would put up with that sort of treatment, these characters aren't a man and a woman. No, the relationship is even more intimate. They're a man and his penis. The scene is from a play called *Hold Until Morning* by Daniel Rudman: I saw it performed at a sex therapy conference in San Francisco a few years ago. *Hold Until Morning* is about every man's first love affair, the love affair that inevitably turns sour – the love affair with his penis. It's a complex, ambiguous, stormy relationship. And the idea of representing a man's emotions and his anatomy as two separate beings is sharply accurate. Many men do feel their penis has a will, a mind of its own. A separate identity. In our society, in most societies, the erect penis is seen as a symbol of masculinity. The strutting, thrusting proof of his manhood. The phallus is the symbol of power, the weapon men use to attract and conquer women and compete with other men.

Man's misfortune is that his penis, the proof of his sexual power, is, in fact, one of the most fragile and vulnerable organs of his body. His weapon is also his weak spot. The window to his inner sexual self, revealing his emotional needs and vulnerability. Therein lies the problem. Men are brought up to feel they shouldn't be emotional, should always be able to perform, always ready and eager. They are not permitted to show vulnerability, not allowed to be nervous, or hesitant or embarrassed or uninterested. Yet all men are these things, sometimes, and it's the penis which gives them away.

It's always there, ready to betray them, to reveal their true feelings to the world and to themselves. That's the point. Men deny their feelings, not only externally but also internally, to themselves. Unable to face their own vulnerability, they cope by denying the penis is part of them. It's easier to treat it as separate, a wilful creature prone to capricious behaviour which says nothing about the man within. An American writer, Jack Litewka, has written an essay called the 'The Socialised Penis' in which he compares the male's relationship with his penis to his relationship with women. He argues that the man is taught to 'objectify' his woman, to see her as composed of sexually arousing parts like breasts or genitals because this makes her less human and hence it is easier for him to assert power over her. 'We do to our penis what we do to females we objectify it, fixate on it and conquer it. In that way we "thingify" our penis, make it "other", so that we can talk about "it" and apologise for "its" behaviour and laugh at "it" as if it were a child on the rambunctious side whom we can't control. So we have confirmed "its" separateness from us. We can even give our penis a name, like John, Thomas or Peter, which states positively to the world that our penis is its own man (and therefore we are not responsible for its actions?).'

So the personification of the penis is actually sad evidence of the need men feel to deny their own emotions, the pressure they feel to perform sexually and their fear of failure. The difficulties they have in tuning into their emotional and sexual feelings and accepting these as normal. It's a defence, and the fact that it's used so often shows how far men still have to go in accepting their sexuality.

The other day I was talking to a group of men about the problems males experience in saying 'no' to sex. There were some sensitive comments from males who did indeed feel under pressure to be interested *all* the time. Then from the other side of the room a wisecrack which broke up the discussion into gales of laughter: 'If I ever said no, my penis would beat me to death.'

It was a great joke but what was this handsome, outgoing young man really saying about the pressures he feels always to be sexual? Like many men, does he feel that whenever he has an erection, he has to have sex? Men I have spoken to find it hard to acknowledge that an erection doesn't always mean you want to share an intimate relationship with a woman. As women, we know that a male's caressing hand can easily bring on those early signs of arousal, a wet vagina, erect nipples. But women are used to saying 'no'. We are permitted to concern ourselves about how we will feel if we do go ahead, how we will feel afterwards. We learn we can ignore our body's natural greedy response and let our emotions apply the brakes.

For men it's not so easy. So often they feel at the mercy of their bodies, their penises. Particularly when they are young, they find it hard to ignore the very obvious signs that their bodies are raring to go . . . whatever butterflies they have in their stomachs, or shaking in their knees.

The erect penis is hard to ignore. It constantly reminds the teenage boy of his sexual urges, distracts him, embarrasses him, forces him to think sexual even when he'd rather just be friends. Over the years I've received so many letters from young men who feel constantly at the mercy of their embarrassing, ever-present erections. They write seeking advice about dampening their sexual drive, stopping themselves from always wanting sex, forcing those damned erections to just go away.

There's a wonderful article called 'Being a Boy' by American author Julius Lester in which he talks of the catastrophe that befalls him the instant he touches the hand of the girl he asks to dance at the teenage party: 'My penis, totally disobeying the lecture I'd give it before we left home, was as rigid as Governor Wallace's jaw would be if I asked for his daughter's hand in marriage.' (It isn't hard to guess Julius Lester is black.) 'God, how I envied girls at that moment. Wherever *it* was on them, it didn't dangle between their legs like an elephant's trunk. No wonder boys talked about nothing but sex. That thing was always there. Every time we went to the john, there *it* was, twitching around like a fat little worm on a fishing hook. When we took baths, it floated in the water like a lazy fish and God forbid we should touch it! It sprang to life like lightning leaping from a cloud. I wished I could cut it off, or at least keep it tucked between my legs, as if it were a tail that had been mistakenly attached to the wrong end. But I was helpless. It was there, with a life and mind of its own, having no other function than to embarrass me.'

'With a life and mind of its own, having no other function than to embarrass me' There it is again. The penis is regarded as a separate identity because it's so hard for the young man to cope with the conflicting demands of his rampant sexual drive and his emotional responses . . . his nervousness, his fear of being rejected or ridiculed, the pressures he feels to compete with other males.

Someone once said, every man's first love is his penis. It's probably true. When young men first discover masturbation they talk of discovering a secret magic toy, a private source of pleasure, and they can't get enough of it. But the relationship quickly becomes more complex, tainted by guilt. Guilt about masturbation remains with many men for most of their lives, eliminating all sensuality from the experience of masturbation. Making it a mechanical act, to be hurried through, a rush towards the relief of a climax.

Sex therapists now believe this attitude towards masturbation is one reason many men have difficulty really enjoying the sensations they experience during lovemaking. They have learnt a mechanistic approach to stimulation where the climax is everything and there's little pleasure along the way. They may have trouble delaying their ejaculation. They have simply never learnt to slow down, tune into the feelings of their body and enjoy the slow, gentle build-up of sensations.

It's an attitude therapists have to work hard to overcome if they are to help men enjoy their sexuality more fully. Bernie Zilbergeld is a sex therapist working in San Francisco who has spent years conducting workshops to help men increase sexual satisfaction. He uses the idea of the penis as a separate person to teach men to tune into their feelings. Zilbergeld has devised a wonderful therapy exercise for men which required them to imagine what it's like to be their penis and then to write a letter from their penis to themselves, the penis owner. The specific questions the man has to answer are 'How does my owner mistreat me?' 'How could my owner treat me better?'

Here are some letters Dr Zilbergeld obtained from the men in his groups, or should I say from the penises of the men in his groups.

'I never feel included. You don't care about me and don't pay any attention to me. Only when you want sex do you show any interest, and then it's only to scream and yell that I better come through for you. Usually you pay more attention to your goddam knees and ankles than to me. Why should I do anything for you? I'd like a little attention and some consideration for my needs. I'd be much more willing to do what you want if I felt that you cared about me. Please pay some attention to me.'

'I'm sick and tired of being called names and threatened. Don't you think I have feelings? I try to do my best and you don't do a damn thing for me or yourself. You get into the weirdest sexual situations that anyone can imagine and expect me to perform. And when I refuse, you get all huffy and start yelling at me. Christ, you don't even like most of the women you want me to screw! And do you ever ask me how I feel about them? Never! Well, the hell with you, Charlie. I'm putting you on notice right now. Either you start treating me with some respect and get into situations that interest both of us, or I'm never going to do anything for you again.'

Zilbergeld uses the letters to teach men to hear what their penises are trying to tell them: 'If your penis doesn't work the way you want it to, remember that it's trying to tell you something. It's not your enemy. It was made for sex, it likes sex. If it's not working the way you like, it's telling you that there is something wrong with the way you are going about sex. If you want better sex, you need to start deciphering your penis's message.'

Talking to men about their relationships with their penises, it's interesting to hear from some who are doing just that. As one man said 'If I am bored during intercourse, my penis is the first to know.' He's realised that his penis is warning him to take note of his feelings. Here, message sent is message received. From the female point of view, I have always been surprised that so often men simply don't read their penises' messages. As a woman I think I have always been very aware that if I'm not lubricated it means that I'm just not in the mood for sex. I may be anxious or stressed or too tired or angry but I know sex isn't going to work for me if I can't get to first base. I might as well take heed of the warning and try to work out what's wrong.

Many men seem to find it harder to acknowledge all is not well. They can't accept their emotions rule their bodies – they're not allowed to admit to such sensitivity. It's just not masculine. So they react to their lack of arousal with anger and look for someone to blame. And there's the enemy. It's that penis who's betrayed them. Listen to this man's description of an unsuccessful sexual encounter: 'I went to bed with a really sex-hungry woman, fearing disaster, and of course it came. Here she was obviously expecting bells to ring and rockets to explode, and all she got was a little fizzle. The look on her face – utter disgust. It was late and she said, "Let's go to sleep'; and turned her back on me. That night I cursed my penis and said – I'll be like this for the rest of my life. I'm a sexual cripple and nobody wants me.' He curses his penis for staying soft, for showing his vulnerability. Other men blame penises for coming too soon or being too small.

That's the saddest part of all. The constant haunting male fear that their penis doesn't come up to scratch, isn't big enough to impress other men in the changerooms, isn't big enough to drive a woman to ecstacy and have her beg for more. Men's magazines have conducted surveys of thousands of men showing that almost all respondents, 'with the exception of the most extraordinarily endowed, expressed doubts about their sexuality based on their penile size.' I have answered so many letters from men who blame their penis size for their partners' lack of enjoyment, lack of orgasms, infidelity, marriage breakdown, their own sexual problems. You name it, the penis gets the blame.

Women often don't realize just how obsessive this male interest in penis size can be. If, like me, you grew up in the 1950s and 1960s you'll have heard of the Chicago Seven, a group of young American radicals charged with conspiracy. One of the group leaders was a radical student leader, Jerry Rubin. Now an author of books about male liberation and male sexuality, Rubin feels his political motivation was at least in part inspired by his concern about penis size: 'For years I felt my penis was too small. Many American males think their penises are not big enough. Bigness is sacred! A big penis means Big Business, and I have been overcompensating since childhood for what I thought was my small penis. I created a Big Image. Whenever I arrived to give a speech in a college town, people greeted me would often say, "We though you were six feet tall." For years, while making love with women, I actually tried to hide my penis from sight. It took acrobatics but it usually worked. The government may think I am a dangerous radical but they don't know the true size of my penis.

After many years of therapy and involvement in men's consciousness-raising groups, Rubin has come to terms with his penis size. He has now learnt to enjoy being touched without worrying whether his woman thinks he's too small. He's learnt to enjoy touching himself, and enjoying his own body, including his penis.

That's the true role of the penis – to give the man pleasure. But for it to do that he has to learn to stop competing with other males, stop comparing, stop putting his penis down. He has to cease seeing his penis as a weapon between his legs and use it to tune into his own emotions and sensitivity. He must learn to enjoy his penis not only when it is strutting and erect but also when it is cuddly and soft and vulnerable. Then and only then can a man fully enjoy his sexuality and sensuality and accept the penis as part, a very special part, of himself.

Sexual Ages of Women

What happens to the sexuality of women as they grow older?
What do we all have to look forward to? The chassis may show
signs of wear and tear but as far as our sexual machinery is concerned, most of us are only just getting into gear in our late
twenties . . . we don't hit our straps until the thirties or forties.
As for the fifties, by then we're cruising effortlessly.

The good news is this: the sex ages of women do not make a
story of gradual decline and fall. Quite the opposite. For most
women sex starts off as a bit of a disappointment and sure, there
are ups and downs, but basically there's steady progress . . . more
enjoyment, more fun, fewer inhibitions, more orgasms, better
orgasms. As one forty-year-old put it; 'Sex – it just gets better
all the time.'

Women have to learn to enjoy sex and that's just what they
are now doing. We know that a woman presently in her twenties
or thirties is far more likely to be sexually responsive than her
mother was at the same age. In fact, research shows the most significant factor in predicting whether a woman is orgasmic is the
decade of her birth. Women born before 1940 have fewer orgasms
than women born before 1950 and so on.

But as well as these changes from generation to generation, we can expect our own sexuality to change and develop as we grow older. There is exciting new research showing just how much women's sexuality develops with age; in time we learn to respond more easily, more often and in many different ways.

'When I was a teenager, I didn't even think much about sex. My head was full of romance and boyfriends: what they thought of me, how far I should let them go. We girls used to laugh about the boys getting all excited, heavy breathing and all that. I can't remember ever thinking of touching myself. I suppose at the back of my mind I was waiting for my prince to awaken me . . . it turned out to be a long wait.'

Teenage girls are often sleeping beauties, blissfully unconscious of the surges of hormones which turn their male companions into Portnoys. While males clutch schoolbags waistlevel to hide the bulging evidence of fantasy-filled minds and remain seated on beaches until Speedos subside, female dreams stop at heaving bosoms and the passionate embrace.

In girls the hormones are churning, the body is gearing itself up for action but the female mind applies the brakes. Here, at the very start of adult female sexuality, we see a pattern emerge which will repeat itself throughout the sexual lives of women. One of the basic differences in the sexuality of men and women is that the female sexual drive is far more easily inhibited than males,' her sexuality more easily distracted, her desire more easily turned off.

And adolescence is a time when young women are bombarded with conflicting messages, do's and dont's which play havoc with budding sexual consciousness. 'Budding' is the right word. The male sexual drive bursts into bloom, the female's awakens slowly. There are few female Portnoys. Approximately 30–40 per cent of women report they either do not masturbate at all or they did not start until after they had a sexual experience that had led to orgasm or intense arousal. The prince came first.

Masturbation, self-stimulation, tells us more about what's happening to teenage girls' sexual interest and sexual response than all the figures on premarital petting and teenage intercourse. The problem is that an awful lot of teenage girls still have sex or grope in the bushes not because they want to, but to hang on to their man, to please him, to be part of the crowd. The frequency of these experiences tells us little about the young woman's own desire or pleasure. In fact here sex often doesn't work very well for the female – there's usually lots of it, but not much pleasure and few orgasms.

For these young women, this is likely to be the pattern for quite some time to come. Coupled by eager partners at the peak of male sexual libido, it's a frustrating time for her when the earth doesn't move. The combination of her own lack of knowledge about what she needs to respond, plus her partner's inexperience and trigger-happy enthusiasm, often brings sexual progress to a standstill.

For some of these females, the search for sexual fulfilment becomes a quest for the magic partner, the magic penis which may hold the key to unlocking their sexuality.

This pattern of a gradual awakening has been the norm and probably still is, but it seems to be changing. Research shows more young women are discovering masturbation, and responding to orgasm through self-stimulation. More are having sex because *they want to* and as a result are enjoying it more.

Besides, we mustn't forget that for every such pattern, there are many exceptions. Judy is now in her late thirties. At age thirteen she first masturbated to orgasm. She was always aware of the pleasure her body could give her. She progressed through petting to intercourse during her late teens and her sexual response was always there: 'I was always sure of my capacity to respond physically,' she says. I could never understand why it seemed to be such a problem for other women. By the time I was thirty I had already experienced over ten years of wonderfully satisfying sexuality.'

By the time women reach their late twenties, early thirties, some will be firing on all cylinders, some will be still finding their way and others will be marking time. Looking at women in this age group we see just how varied women's lives have become – how wide their choice of options. Once, most women in their late twenties were already married with children. Now they're everywhere, in every kind of relationship: single, settled with one man, still playing the field, married but childless, divorced, single mums.

There is room for sexual growth in all these circumstances, for learning experiences which contribute to a woman's understanding of her sexuality and her ability to respond. There's no predicting the best way. Sometimes a one-night stand with the right man can open new doors, sometimes it will slam them shut for years. The comfort of a steady relationship may free inhibitions, sometimes it stifles and snuffs out all desire. It's a time ripe with possibilities but there's one option most of us still choose at this time which affects our sexuality more than most others combined – motherhood.

Usually, of course, this is preceded by pregnancy, a state of grace which can have quite unpredictable effects on sexuality. Some sail through it, their sexual response totally unaffected or even enhanced. I have friends who, with great creativity and enthusiasm, frolicked their way through the entire nine months.

Others turn off – for all sorts of reasons. When pregnancy is uncomfortable – with constant nausea, fatigue, depression, sex is the last thing on your mind. Some women are nervous of harming the foetus – anxiety dampens their ardour. Hormones may play a part. My obstetrician believes the extra androgens floating around when the foetus is male can increase the female libido. He uses the effect of pregnancy on sex drive to predict the sex of the child. He's not always right but he usually beats the odds.

Then there's body image. Some women revel in their swelling tummies and fuller breasts. Others feel unattractive, undesirable. The male response plays a part and that is equally varied. It's also very strange to be treated like mother earth instead of a sex object. No wolf whistles, no sexy leers – and for some women, a huge drop in sexual confidence and self esteem.

This is just the beginning. Then there's the legacy. Often considerable wear and tear on the old chassis – less firm breasts, changes in nipple colour, stretch marks. Even with exercise, healthy diet, it's still a matter of luck just how much your body will bear witness to the extraordinary changes which have taken place. Some accept and enjoy this change to a mature, womanly figure, others lose confidence. How you feel about yourself and the way you look is such a vital ingredient in relaxed lovemaking. The woman who, despite her husband's reassurance, constantly hides her wrinkled tummy may have a hard time regaining her former ease with her body during sex. Yet women of any age, with or without pregnancy and childbirth, must learn to like the way they are and accept changes as they occur. Perhaps we should all take heed of that ghastly male joke about not looking at the mantelpiece while stoking the fire. I know it's not meant to be complimentary but mutual stoking is what it's all about.

The effect of these changes pales in comparison with the other devastating consequence of pregnancy – children. 'Mothersuckers', they call them. And even the most devoted mum will acknowledge the stress, the fatigue, the draining effect these wonderful creatures have on their mums – particularly when it's the first time around. Early motherhood tops the polls in most of the lists of causes of libido loss in women. Research shows loss of sexual drive, decrease in orgasm frequency and marital disharmony as mothers struggle to cope with their new role. Even that most sensuous of experiences, breastfeeding, may detract from the more active sexual libido necessary for responding with a man. The mother, constantly locked in intimate embrace with her child, may feel little need for more overt sexual play. Again these are generalisations and for other women, particularly women fully sexually responsive before the birth of their first child, motherhood may cause few problems and childbirth itself may even be an erotic experience.

Luckily most of us, however shell-shocked, eventually recover our sanity and our sexuality . . . and there may even be bonuses. Pregnancy may enhance the female's capacity for orgasms by increasing the number of blood vessels in the genital area. As blood flow is essential for arousal and orgasm, sometimes, bingo it all starts to happen . . . Of course, it's not always great timing. Imagine learning to reach orgasm for the first time and whenever you just get going you hear that plaintive cry from the nursery.

It shows just how much sexual response is dependent on the woman's circumstances – her relationship with her husband or lover, the other stresses and demands on her, her general health, her level of fatigue.

Sex doesn't exist on its own. It's part of everyday life and is affected by it. So the career woman struggling to cope with increasing job responsibilities, pressures at work, financial hassles, will also find her sexual response waxes and wanes. But the miracle is that our sexuality not only survives all these ups and downs but through it all gradually grows and blossoms.

Some fascinating unpublished research by Mary Jo Sholty in the US analysed the orgasmic histories of women aged from eighteen to fifty-nine. She found 97 per cent of the women interviewed reported their ability to climax had changed over time. For three-quarters of the women the quality of their orgasms improved – they lasted longer, were more intense, easier to achieve, more frequent. Most women gradually had learned to respond to varying types of stimulation, initially responding, for instance, to direct clitoral stimulation only and then to stimulation during intercourse. They also learn to experience their orgasms in different locations, reporting both clitoral sensations, vaginally-located orgasms and combinations of the two.

The major impression is of change – women's response changing over time in all sorts of ways, a gradual movement onwards but also plenty of fits and starts. Almost all the women went through periods when they responded less easily, were less interested and then things improved.

And what was it that produced these changes? The overwhelming message was that the women themselves changed: 'It's me. Sure, outside influences are important. But the bottom line is . . . if I want it, I can have it. If I don't, I can't. But it wasn't always like that either. You have to know how to do it and want to. My attitude is so much better. It's terrific.'

'You can have all the right things – partner, setting, stimulation – if you aren't into it, you're not going to have orgasm. I know my attitude about orgasm, the whole sex scene almost cost me my marriage.'

'It's mostly up to us. Society, parents or what-have-you stuck us with some real hang-ups, but it's up to us whether we want to complain or do something about it.'

'Sometimes you have to change how you think. Sure I was inhibited having sex with the kids around, but I got tired of waiting until it was time for them to visit Grandma. So I learned to do it with them around. They survived. So did we.'

The women who have travelled the greatest distance are our midlife women, the women in their forties and fifties. These are the women who grew into adulthood before the so-called 'sexual revolution'. They started off their sexual lives incredibly ignorant, full of expectations but unprepared to achieve these dizzy heights; 'It was terrible at first, just terrible. He wanted me to be a virgin – that was very important to him before we were married – and he also wanted me to be skilled in bed right from the start. When I think of it now, I feel outraged because it wasn't even our fault. We were just playing our parts, like puppets on strings.'

These women have come a long way. For anyone interested in women's lives and how they are changing, I recommend an absolutely superb book: *Women Of a Certain Age – The Midlife Search For Self* by Lillian B. Rubin (Harper, New York, 1981). This book is an inspiring account of the changing lives of 160 women, interviewed at length about their hopes, aspirations, career, families, relationships, sex.

It shows dramatically just how much sex has changed over the past decade for most of these women and how excited they are to discover their sexuality after years of frustration and disappointment. 'I'm enjoying sex more than I ever did in my life before, maybe more than I ever thought I could.'

Incidentally, just as the body learns to respond and climax more easily, it appears it can also grow rusty through lack of use. Research is sketchy but certainly in males it appears sexual response can suffer as a result of long periods of sexual abstinence. The best means of ensuring everything keeps working well throughout your life is the regular use of your sexual equipment.

In the midst of all this good news, there can be problems. Of any group I have talked about, it is in this one that we see the greatest male fallout, the strongest reaction from male partners to this expanding female sexual potential. It's hardly surprising. The male partners, the husbands of these women, also started their sexual lives with quite different expectations about sex and about female sexuality. And now, at a time when their own sexuality is changing, calming down a little, their assumptions about sex, about the women they have made love to for ten, twenty years, are turned upside down.

It frightens them. Their women, brought up to nurture males, to stroke male egos, know it well and suppress their own needs rather than kick their men when they are down; 'There's nothing worse than to push him and have him unable to perform. If he fails, it causes more problems than it's worth. It's a shame because I feel deprived now when I never would have before. But I worry more about him than I do about myself. So I just wait for him to ask me. That's easier all around.' And; 'It makes me furious that just when I become a real sexual being, he cops out. Oh, that's not fair, is it? It's not his fault. Sex has always been so important to him, and I know how hard it must be not to be able to do it all the time. I guess he was what you'd call a sexual athlete until a few years ago, when that all changed. I feel very badly for him, I really do. But I guess I can't help feeling bad for myself, too. It just seems like one of life's rotten tricks.'

Yes, it is one of life's rotten tricks and as *Women Of A Certain Age* shows, the male reaction is not just a response to changes in his wife's sexuality. These midlife women are moving out in all sorts of other ways, developing careers, acquiring education, new confidence and independence. When the man cops out from sex, loses interest or becomes impotent, he may be reacting to a lot more than just a sexual threat.

Of course, it isn't always like this. Sometimes a woman's sexual awakening is an unexpected bonus for the man, a reward for years of patience, gentle encouragement. His slowing down, his new ability to delay ejaculation can be just what the doctor ordered . . . and what a thrill it can be for them both.

And some women, many women in this age group, are still unable to take advantage of a cultural climate that offers permission for more sexual freedom they ever dreamed of: 'I wish I could be sexually free like the kids, but I can't. It just doesn't work for me. Too many years of repression I suppose, and too many lessons and I learned too well.'

These are complex patterns, influenced by so many factors. There is menopause – like pregnancy – a complex phenomenon which influences women in many different ways. I have talked about husbands, about steady relationships but have not even looked at the effects of the strangers who pass through the sexual lives of women.

What happens to a woman's sexuality when her sexual awakening causes her eye to stray, when she moves outside the confines of her marriage?

Research shows that more and more women are having extramarital affairs – no longer is philandering confined to males. Double standards regarding attitudes towards male and female fidelity are slowly changing – what's good for the goose in increasingly seen as okay for the gander as well. Yet there are differences between men and women in their attitude towards extra-marital relationships. When questioned about their motivation in having affairs, men are more likely to mention a desire for sexual adventure, a need for variety, whereas with women the motivation is more likely to be emotional and sexual dissatisfaction with their marriage. This means that when a married women does have an affair it is *far* more likely to pose a threat to the marriage – her affair is a distress signal, a sign that the marriage is already in trouble. Men, on the other hand, really mean it when they plaintively plead 'but it didn't mean anything'.

There are so many complex factors involved here that it is extremely difficult to begin to cover all the possible milestones in the sexual lives of women. To use such a broad brush to describe the intricacies of the sex ages of women does such a disservice to our individuality, our uniqueness.

Perhaps it is fitting that there's so little room left to describe the group whose sexuality is ignored. Older women, say sixties and over have an even more difficult job than the preceding generation to throw off the repression that existed during their early lives. With this group, more than any other, we need to be aware of sexuality in its broadest context, of all the possible means of sexual expression, of the importance of touching, of intimacy, of closeness. The sad fact is that many women will end up spending a considerable period of their later life on their own, with little or no opportunity of establishing new relationships. Elderly widowed and divorced women far outnumber the available men in their age group. To make matters worse, the older men who find themselves left on their own will often seek partners not from amongst their peers but from the large number of single women twenty, even thirty years younger. The tragedy of the older woman is not only that the odds are against her but she often feels under pressure to deny or hide her need for intimacy let alone sexual pleasure. While the older man does run the risk of being seen as a 'dirty old man' if he reveals his sexual needs, a man seen with a woman twenty years his junior is greeted with a grin and a certain amount of grudging respect. An older woman known to be seeking sex is regarded as comic or indecent, particularly if she chooses a younger partner.

Yet both males and females do remain sexual throughout their lives. When, after a twenty or thirty-year marriage, a husband or wife dies, the grieving partner is left to deal with not only unfulfilled needs for intimacy and closeness but also basic sexual desires which don't magically disappear just because there is no longer an acceptable outlet for those needs. For an older generation raised in a more conservative era, it may be very difficult to come to terms with one obvious solution to the physical need, masturbation. Many older men and women turn to masturbation at this stage in their lives, but do so plagued by guilt: 'Sometimes when I touch myself, I feel better and can go to sleep. Other times I'm sadder and I cry, thinking of how alone I am. When I go for a long time trying and it doesn't help at all, I think of how angry my mother would be at me . . . she always told me I'd get a rash all over, and people would know.' This woman is in her seventies – her mother has been dead for over thirty years.

In one respect, women on their own do have an advantage over the equivalent males, they are more likely to be supported by a network of friends and relatives, to maintain close contact with children and grandchildren. Research on patterns of friendship show that women are far better at establishing close intimate relationships with other women and as friends pass out of their lives, they continue to make new contacts and find new means of support and comfort.

It is at this stage that all the hard female work of achieving and maintaining social skills, nurturing friendships, caring for other people, pays off as the older woman uses these skills to keep in touch with the world. The male, who all his life has left the task of social lubrication to his wife, his women, now finds it harder to maintain friendships and make new ones. Male friendships often fade away and are never replaced leaving the older men increasingly isolated.

And when older people do meet and form new relationships – we often make it hard for those relationships to develop. Many retirement villages, old people's homes and nursing homes have antiquated rules about overnight visits, segregated rooms and so on, robbing residents of their privacy, treating them like children requiring constant supervision. Many of us *are* very uncomfortable about the notion of our parents and our parents' generation still finding each other sexually attractive. We snigger and giggle and make hurtful comments – we don't know how to cope when the aging father brings his new girlfriend to stay for a visit, we don't know how to introduce her to our friends or whether to offer separate rooms. Often our discomfort, our censure is sufficient to stifle a budding romance – instead of offering encouragement, we allow our anxiety and social embarrassment to thwart their chances.

Yet all this may soon change. In a society with an increasing greying population, more attention is being paid to the sexual and social needs of the elderly and there has already been a positive shift in attitudes. More elderly people are risking raised eyebrows and seeking out new partners and the rewards are already as this sixty-nine-year old shows when she describes her new romance with a seventy-six-year old man: 'Remember our faces may be lined and our silhouettes bulging but – as someone else has said, the heart has no wrinkles. We thrill to the surprise of what's below the neck, even in septuagenarian bodies, as we find cool and firm shoulders, smooth, pink buttocks and velvety thighs. We find a treasure chest of sensations and sampling a few at a time, smack our lips at the goodies on our future agenda.'

Would that we all could embark on the evening of our sexual lives with such enthusiasm.

New Demands of Parenthood

It's Never Easy

*I*t was all hard enough before psychologists got into the act. The awesome responsibility of parenthood has always guaranteed years of sleepless nights and exhausted days, the tedious rituals of feeding, bathing, teeth cleaning, agonising battles over discipline and homework. It's never been easy but, left to muddle through on their own, most parents did a pretty good job.

Then along came the experts, the psychiatrists, child psychologists, all eagerly searching for evidence of failed parenting. Bedwetting, stammering, autism, teenage pregnancy, adult fears and phobias; you name it, they blamed the parents. All parents were found more or less guilty of having failed their children. Am I doing what is right? Am I doing enough? Am I doing too much? Parents are constantly bombarded with conflicting evidence and contradictory information, feeding their guilt and making all but the most confident parents a little nervous.

Often the experts turn out to be wrong, sometimes they even change their minds – yesterday's prescription for good parenting is thrown away, to be replaced by fresh rules, new mistakes we all can make in rearing our children. It wasn't so long ago that psychiatrists swapped theories on what it was that caused a son or daughter to turn into a homosexual – one week it was the smothering mother, the next, the absent dad. And when the professionals finally let parents off the hook and swung back to some vague biological explanation, the parents were left with guilt. However much they are reassured, there's always the niggling fear 'perhaps I shouldn't have let him learn to knit, to let her climb trees'. There are always new fears, new problems that we never suspected could affect our children. Like child abuse. We all knew about the man in the park with boiled lollies, we'd warned them about dark alleys and accepting lifts from strangers. And now we learn the real danger comes not from the unknown but from familiar territory . . . the next door neighbour, the relative, the friend. It's a thought that most of us find hard to accept. How can we protect children from dangers that form part of the world they know and love?

Increasingly parents are dealing with these new and complex problems, not as a united team but on their own – as single mothers or divorced parents with children as their sole remaining link. How difficult it becomes to deal with these issues when you are still bound up with the pain of separation, still mourning a failed marriage. Often the responsibility is left to one parent, while the other is increasingly cut adrift from the daily life of the children. Sometimes it's just too hard – the isolated parent opts out, walks away. But most try in their own way to battle through – for the sake of the children.

Despite all the complexities, the new doubts facing parents today, we cling to the uncertain rewards of being a parent. And luckily we find them still there.

Lone Fathers

David's two boys, aged seventeen and fifteen, have lived for the past five years with his ex-wife in Queensland. David sees them whenever he can; they stay with him in Sydney during all school holidays and he keeps in regular contact by telephone and letter. Last year Father's Day came and went without the customary telephone call from the boys. David, puzzled, contacted his ex-wife to find out why. He then learnt that for the past eleven days, his elder son had been lying unconscious in a hospital bed following a motor cycle accident.

That one really gets to you. Not even to *know* for eleven days. To eat breakfast, go to work, make love, get drunk, to live for almost two weeks without knowing your son was in a coma. Not even to be given a chance to grieve, to care. Every parent, mother or father, imagining themselves in that situation must feel the same shiver up the spine. Yet this is simply an extreme example of a tragedy which occurs just about every time a marriage ends in Australia today. For most men, the end of a marriage signals the end of their chance to be active parents to their children.

It is the mothers who end up the single parents, struggling to bring up children on their own. Through a combination of factors they are denied their best possible source of support, the ideal help with child care – the children's father. The list of reasons is endless: the woman's anger and hurt; the father's indifference; the court system; society's assumptions about fathering. Each of these requires explanation but the result is overwhelming.

Only a tiny minority of men ever consider seeking custody of their children, fewer still make the attempt. Of these a surprising 50 per cent succeed. Where possible, courts award fathers access to their children, varying usually from a few hours a week to a weekend each fortnight. In most cases, access doesn't work. The father loses touch with his children. As a *very* rough estimate perhaps one in five divorced fathers has anything but a token relationship with his children. It's a tragedy, for the men themselves, the mothers who need their help, the children who lose their fathers. But it's also a complex issue which touches raw nerves in so many of us, where our assumptions, our emotions so often overrule our better judgement.

I should declare my interest. For years I lived with a man, I married a man who fought to make sure the end of his marriage didn't mean the end of his relationship with his two children. The major obstacle he encountered was the assumption that he was a little odd to care so much. There was always the charge, rarely voiced, that perhaps it would be better if he just dropped out of their lives.

Now I have my own child and can see the other side. There was the time, the first time my babysitter took my two-week-old baby for a walk to give me a chance to have a nap. When she returned after an hour, long enough, she thought, for me to have a good rest, I was pacing the streets in my dressing gown, his father dispatched to search with the car. There's nothing rational about that fierce instinct of a mother to protect, to hold her children near. Now I can feel what it must do to a woman to have to share her children with someone who has caused her pain, someone who is no longer her friend, her husband.

It's not easy to be sensible. It's not easy to put aside such emotions and really think about what is in 'the best interests of the child', to use the lawyers' phrase. But surely we would all, mothers, fathers and children, be better off if divorced fathers were not excluded from their families. Yet the teething problems are immense.

'You do all the work, the cleaning and washing. Getting up in the middle of the night. Fixing runny noses. Then every week you send them off all polished and pretty and they come back grubby and exhausted from having a lovely time. Laden with the gifts you can't afford to give them, bubbling with talk of expensive outings, eating out, treats galore. He gives them all this and then it takes you ages to turn them back into normal children. It's just not fair . . .'

No, it's not fair. The Responsibility Mum and the Entertainment Dad. The lone mother weighed down with the relentless responsibility of caring for children on her own envies the freedom of the father to walk away at the end of the day. She must cope with whatever slice of the financial cake that is hers after the lawyers have carved up the loot of their marriage. There's often little left for those treats that only money can buy.

It's a familiar story but there's another side. Listen to two fathers: 'I'm allowed to have Peter for five hours a fortnight. I live almost one hour's drive away from his mother's home, so for me to take him to my place means that he spends the first hour of his time with me strapped in the back of the car. I don't want him to see his father just as a fellow who takes him out once a fortnight and gives him a good time. I want him to see how I live, expose him to my life. What else can I do . . . go to the beach, go to the shops. People say you shouldn't just make it an entertainment thing, but there's not much else you can do.' (Andrew, father of Peter, aged 2).

'I wasn't allowed to take Sam home if Mary, my girlfriend, was there. Sometimes if I wanted to go home she would duck out and hide, but most of the time I was one of those Disneyland fathers. There's a limit to the number of places you can take a child – Luna Park, Marineland. We used to eat a lot at MacDonalds. You feel sort of strange when you go out on your own with your son. Eventually he would get so exhausted he would fall asleep. All this running around. It makes the child think you are some sort of freak or weirdo and don't have a normal life of your own. When you only have one day you never want to chastise them because you are afraid they will think you are some sort of ogre. It was a nightmare. I often felt like giving up. You get driven to it in the end . . .' (Michael, father of Sam, aged 3).

Both these fathers divorced when their children were tiny, less than three years old. They are part of an increasing group of fathers who are awarded only a few hours contact with their children each week or each fortnight. When a divorce occurs involving babies or toddlers, the needs of the father are swamped by a wave of opinion, backed by so-called 'experts', intent on promoting the sanctity of the mother-child relationship. There is an assumption, rarely questioned, that the mother is the only person capable of caring for a child of that age and that any separation from the mother could damage the child. Even recently published books on divorce warn of the emotional dangers of separation, even for a few hours at a time, from a mother – a danger which is felt to be particularly acute when dealing with very young children, babies or pre-schoolers.

You have only to think for a moment to realise such thinking no longer conforms to current practice. Our society accepts that no mother could or should be expected to live for two years without an occasional break from her children. Even the most devoted mum will sometimes use a babysitter or call in the relatives to take time off to recover her sanity. In fact, almost 45 per cent of pre-school mothers have their children minded for periods of up to forty hours per week. Only one-third of mothers claim to be the sole carers for their pre-school children. Whether or not we approve of this trend away from twenty-four-hour-a-day motherhood, that's how we now live. The evidence is that overall it isn't doing children nor their mothers any harm. In fact, recent research by Dr Chris Tennant, Associate Professor at Sydney University, shows the greatest danger to the woman's mental health is the isolation of constant motherhood.

But back in the divorce courts, the wheels of change turn very slowly indeed. Much emphasis is still placed on dangers of separation of a young child from his or her mother – whatever evidence there is to the contrary outside in the real world. Lawyers and counsellors still quote from child psychologists such as Bowlby whose 1940s work on maternal deprivation of children has since been discredited by child development experts the world over.

It's a farce and most fathers see straight through it. They know that their children are not being cared for all the time by the mothers. They know their ex-wives are happy to use grandparents, friends, child-care facilities to give them the time they need for themselves. 'One family court counsellor told me that until the child was five, he shouldn't stay overnight away from his familiar home. Yet the counsellor knew and I knew that Peter often stays with his grandparents for a whole weekend. That's not his home. My home could become familiar to him – if they gave us a chance.' (Andrew).

'When I went to court the judge said he couldn't understand why I wanted so much time with Kate; after all the child was so young. He actually said he thought it would be better if I saw her less frequently. Can you imagine that? I had moved from Melbourne to Sydney to be near her and here was this judge suggesting shorter access time. The counsellors often reinforced my wife's feeling that I already had too much time with Kate. They said you should consider yourself lucky you've got these two hours because we know of many cases where people have only one hour every three weeks'. (George, father of Kate, aged 2).

The truth is that whatever courts or counsellors try to do to encourage mothers to allow fathers access to their children, the power lies with the mother – the parent who almost always has custody. This power is often misused – for very good reasons. The woman is being asked to share her infant children with her ex-husband precisely when her wounds are most raw. With babies, with toddlers, she is probably somewhat nervous of even letting them out of her sight. Yet now she is asked to hand them over to a man for whom she probably has very mixed emotions – anger, disappointment, lack of trust, bitterness, regret. It's a tall order.

Most women find it hard to cope with the weekly or fortnightly upset to their routine as the children are whisked away and then return withdrawn, upset, angry. And late. Is the dinner ruined? No matter, he's probably stuffed them full of chips again. The painful handover, tears, sullen looks. The women are the ones left to comfort the child whose Teddy is left at daddy's, who doesn't understand why daddy doesn't live here anymore.

So women wield their power and collect evidence of bedwetting and nightmares. For the lawyers, they catalogue the times he was late or just forgot. They tell of his girlfriends, his drinking. Niggle over delivery times – five minutes becomes a cause for war. They force him to stay in the car, just beep the horn and wait for the children to appear. He is never invited to the kindy Christmas party nor speechdays, nor birthday parties. He never meets their teachers, never knows their friends. He remains a stranger. And he gives up. Many men do give up. Research by the Australian Family Court shows that 77 per cent of children have contact fortnightly or more six months after separation, two to three years later, this figure is down to 66 per cent. Access does tend to drop off over time, particularly when the rules regarding access are imposed by a court rather than mutually agreed upon by the parents.

Some fathers do re-enter their children's lives at a later time, when passions have cooled. But will their children still know them, still feel connected? The problems *can* be less severe when children are older, or when there are older siblings to help a small child to feel secure. At least they remember when dad was at home.

It's when the children are young, the family just begun, that the father is at most risk of being excluded. What we must realise is this is a growing group of fathers, a trend we cannot ignore. In Australia today more couples are delaying having children until a few years after they marry, and more couples are divorcing earlier in their marriage. The result is more divorces involving fewer and younger children: babies, toddlers, children under five. We're presently seeing the effect of the 1940–60s baby boom and according to Dr Ray King of the University of Sydney, this will mean many more divorces involving such young children, at least for the next ten years.

All the more reason for those involved in divorce, judges, lawyers and counsellors, to look very carefully at their assumptions regarding the best solutions for these young divided families. The trouble is these experts' main experience is with parents at war, the dispute, custody cases where the battle still rages. These decision makers, the advice-givers, never see the families who achieve their own peace, who work out for themselves what is best for their children.

Not so easy? No, but there's some research which may be relevant here. A fascinating study of divorced fathers by Americans Kristine Rosenthal and Harry Keshet is contained in the book *Fathers Without Partners* (Rowman and Littlefield, New Jersey, 1981). This research found that the more contact there was between the father and children, the more the divorced parents *shared* the child rearing, the more the mother and father tended to respect each other as parents and turn to each other for support. The fathers who saw their children once a week or less reported a great deal of conflict with their ex-spouses, particularly regarding child-rearing techniques. Less than half of these fathers saw their ex-wives as competent parents. The more contact fathers had with their children, the more likely they were to describe their ex-wives a good mothers.

In the light of these findings, the present policy regarding access involving young children is a recipe for disaster. A few hours once a week or a fortnight provides sufficient contact to maintain the rage of the mother without ever allowing the parents to develop mutual respect through a better understanding of each other's problems. Okay, so some never will, however much contact they have. But if co-operation with the non-custodial parent was stressed as a factor in determining whom should have custody, we might see a change in attitude. Plenty of fathers today are proving it is perfectly possible for fathers to raise children, from infancy onwards.

The saddest thing is that most men give up without even knowing what they are missing. The women complain, 'he was never interested before', remembering the times he arrived home after the children were in bed, or played golf all weekend. But it's not easy for a man to emerge from behind the newspaper. It's not always his fault he hid there while the family carried on around him. Women jealously guard their mothering skills, their competence in the home.

There *are* explanations for all the games divorced parents play, for all the wounds they inflict on each other and on their children. When they remain in contact, when the fathers hang in there, many learn to understand and become friends. And *their* children are the ones most likely to emerge unscathed. But for this to happen, somehow men must be helped not to lose heart. A few hours in Luna Park isn't the answer.

Children and Sexual Assault

Your six-year-old daughter comes home late from school and tells you about the stranger who stopped his car near her bus stop and asked for directions. When she approached the car to tell him where to go, he opened the car door, unzipped his trousers and tried to get her to touch him. You would believe her, wouldn't you? You can imagine the fear hitting the pit of your stomach and your instant desire to protect her.

Now imagine your reaction if your small daughter told you her uncle had rubbed his tummy against her. Would you tell her she must be imagining it? Would it occur to you that a member of your own family could be making a sexual approach to your child?

Probably not. We are just not used to thinking that way. We are taught to be frightened of strangers in the park, or men with boiled lollies lurking in the bushes. We can't bring ourselves to be suspicious of the nice man who delivers the groceries, or the next door neighbour who teaches the children cricket, let alone our cousins, father, brothers, husbands. So we ignore the signs, the children's cries for help. When Jacki doesn't want her brother to babysit for her any more, we tell her not to be so silly. When a thirteen-year-old girl stops eating, has nightmares, starts playing up in school, we think she's just showing signs of puberty. When a five-year-old draws stick figures with large penises and starts talking about sex, we blame her rough friends and think about changing her school. When girls tell us about a friend whose daddy gets into bed and touches her every night, we are surprised and shocked but never think she may be trying to tell us about herself, and her own daddy.

It is our innocence, our inability to believe the children that places them at risk and allows the sexual abuse of perhaps hundreds of thousands of children in this country each year – abuse by their own families and by their adult friends. It has only been in the last few years that some of the taboos have been lifted and women have started talking about the sexual abuse they experienced as children and the effects this had on their lives. You must have read their stories. For every published case of incest or sexual abuse, there are thousands of similar experiences that go unreported. Talk to your friends. In any group of women, there is always someone who remembers an adult man, older brother, cousin, who tried to get her to touch him, or crept into her bedroom at night to look at her body or rub himself against her. There is always a woman who remembers being held tight on male laps conscious of the bulge of an erection. And there is often a woman who has tried to forget the pain and fear of probing fingers in her vagina, or even of intercourse, often repeated night after night, or whenever mum went out to work.

The evidence is now accumulating and it is now estimated that perhaps one in four children experience some sort of sexual assault by the time they are eighteen. Throughout Australia, notifications to welfare authorities of alleged child abuse are increasing every year. In New South Wales since 1980, notifications have doubled each year. The more we talk about the problem, the more people are willing to admit it is happening. The victims are mainly girls (perhaps 90 per cent) and the offenders mainly male. Unlike rape, which usually occurs on just one occasion, the child victim of a sexual assault is usually abused over and over again, often for years on end. When we talk about sexual assault we are not just talking about rape or actual intercourse, often it's a far more subtle approach involving the man exposing himself or asking to be touched, or looking at or feeling his female victim. The girl may be threatened with violence or even physically abused to force her to participate but more often it is simply a case of her just being asked or bribed to do something by someone older than her, an adult who tells her that there's nothing wrong with what they are doing.

The interesting thing is that she usually doesn't believe him. Most child victims of sexual assault *know* that there's something wrong – their instincts tell them that something strange is going on. They want to tell someone but they are afraid. What are they afraid of? Sometimes they have been told not to tell and they fear being punished if they tell the secret. Even very young children have often learnt that anything to do with sex and those hidden-private parts of their body is regarded as naughty and wicked and they worry that, if they tell, they will be the ones who get into trouble. They know instinctively that they have been involved in something taboo. Saddest of all is the fact that often the child doesn't tell because she (or he) knows she won't be believed.

All too often when a child tries to seek help that is precisely what happens. Victims of sexual assault frequently tell stories of being punished or told off by the person they attempted to tell about the sexual assault. One American study of victims found that 63 per cent had never told anyone about the sexual exploitation until they were interviewed by the researcher. The rest of the girls tried to tell . . . their mothers (68 per cent), siblings, other relatives or friends (26 per cent), teachers (2 per cent), police (2 per cent), but their stories weren't always well received. A quarter of the girls weren't believed – it was assumed they were making it up. It is hard to imagine how a four or five-year-old girl could make up stories about a man putting his penis between her thighs. When she talks about such things she doesn't even understand what is really happening – how could she know unless someone, an adult was showing her? Freud was the one who really gave this myth credibility with his theories about girls fantasising about incest with their fathers and since then generations of psychologists and therapists have chosen to dismiss stories of child abuse as fantasy. It is only now that many of these experts are beginning to realise the damage they have caused children by teaching their parents not to believe them. Children don't make up such stories – by calling them liars, we contribute to their abuse.

Back to the American study. Apart from the children who weren't believed, often the person the victim told expressed hostility, *not* towards the offender but to the girl herself. She was blamed for the offence. We all know it happens with rape victims . . . she asked for it, they all say, she shouldn't have worn that mini-skirt, or accepted that lift. But a five-year-old child? A thirteen-year-old girl? Asking for it?

Apart from the general disbelief and secrecy that surrounds the whole question of child abuse, the concept of the seductive child is one of the myths which places the child most at risk of continued abuse. Little girls are encouraged to behave in coquettish, winsome ways towards adult males, particularly their daddies. 'Isn't she sweet,' they say as she clambers on to daddy's knee. 'She wraps him around her little finger.' Girls quickly learn to behave seductively towards adult males . . . it wins them smiles, affection, presents. It is this behaviour which allows males to excuse themselves from responsibility for their sexual actions.

The father, the uncle, the adult male discovered molesting a young girl, frequently claims in his defence that he was unable to control his sexual response to her seductive ways. He may claim she enjoyed the experience or even that she made the first sexual approach by teasing him or touching him. Our court system supports this notion of the seductive child with some of the State laws covering sexual assault requiring the child to prove she did not consent to the assault. The fact that consent is *ever* an issue perpetuates the notion that the child could be responsible for the assault and effectively lets men off the hook. Many of the welfare workers working with victims of assault believe it is crucial that we get rid of this type of thinking. Men must be taught that they are *always* responsible for their sexual actions in situations involving minors however the child behaves towards them. It is essentially a power issue similar to the doctor who seduces his patients. Children or young girls aren't ever in a situation to give consent freely – they are emotionally too much at risk.

The worst aspect of this shifting the blame on to the victim is the effect it has on the woman herself. Most victims do blame themselves – they feel guilty because they know they have been involved in something taboo, they feel guilty because they haven't been able to stop it happening, they feel guilty because they may well have become aroused and enjoyed the sexual experience. The point is that the child's reactions at the time simply aren't relevant to the issue of male responsibility. *He* was the one who should have said 'no' and the last thing the victim needs is more guilt and blame heaped upon her.

Part of the problem is also tied up with myths about male sexuality. We are taught to believe that males are rampantly randy creatures who once aroused are unable to control their sexual actions. It's a line we learn as teenagers when young males try to persuade girls to give into them by arguing they will be in agony if left unrelieved. Later, when the man married, he traditionally was regarded as having bought the sexual services of his wife through his marriage contract. Of course, we no longer believe wives have to service their husbands. These days women are allowed to say 'no' but old attitudes die hard and often when it is discovered that a child is being sexually abused by a father, the blame is shifted to the mother.

It is extraordinary, reading through the literature on child abuse, to note how often the experts find excuses for the male's behaviour in the fact 'that he was sexually estranged from his partner'. Psychologists have built up a picture of what they call the 'dysfunctional family' where problems in the relationship between husband and wife is seen as a contributing cause of the sexual abuse problem. In terms of protecting children, this type of thinking is extremely dangerous, because it shifts blame and responsibility away from the offender and allows him to justify his actions. For as long as men can tell themselves they have a right to turn to children if they are denied sex by their wives, *and* have this excuse supported by psychologists, psychiatrists and the courts, the more likely it is that men won't exercise the restraint needed to stop themselves drifting into a sexual abuse situation.

In fact, research on incestuous fathers shows they aren't being sexually deprived by their wives. Nicholas Groth, a psychologist who has had extensive experience with incestuous fathers showed the men were having sexual relations with their daughters or sons, in addition to, rather than instead of, their wives. Those offenders who confined their sexual activity to children, did so through choice. There was no one for whom no other opportunity for sexual gratification existed. Of course if you think logically about it, there is *never* no opportunity for sexual gratification – males are always capable of providing themselves with sexual relief if necessary. It is time we broke down the myth that males *need* sexual gratification and women, perhaps even children, are forced to provide it.

Men who abuse children usually don't start out seeking sexual relief. It appears that men often just drift into a sexual abuse situation when they find themselves becoming sexually aroused in normal family interaction with their children. I say 'normal' family interaction, but in fact the physical contact many males have with their children isn't always so normal or desirable as it often involves the father doing things to the child that she may not really enjoy. I often think back to situations when someone, an older person, was tickling me when I was a child. I *hated* being tickled and used to cry desperately for someone to stop them tormenting me and I remember adults laughing at me while they simply watched it happen. I've noticed this with my own children and always try to stop people from inflicting this type of 'rough-house' play on children who don't enjoy it but it is hard to assert yourself. I have watched men play games throwing my young child in the air and instinctively wanted to stop them, but it's accepted that these are the ways men relate to children. Obviously, in themselves, these actions are harmless, but they set up a situation where children learn that adults do things to them they don't like or which frighten them, and other adults, the mothers like me, just sit back and watch it all happening. Does this stop them seeking help when something worse is happening?

If you talk to mothers of incest victims, they sometimes tell you that their instinct told them that something was not right about the way the father forced his daughter to sit on his knee, or spent so long reading bedtime stories to her. But when they questioned their husbands they were told not to be so silly. 'Surely I know how to treat my own daughter?' Perhaps we all are too used to not trusting our own judgement and too afraid of putting our foot down when something just doesn't seem right. Often the mother will simply not be aware that anything is happening to her child. She, like the rest of us, simply doesn't believe that such a thing could happen in her family and this belief helps keep the incest or abuse out of her sight, and out of her mind. One of the other myths about incest and sexual abuse is the 'collusive' wife, the woman whom it is assumed knows what's going on and just doesn't choose to see. Mothers are accused of abandoning their child to go out to work, are held responsible for the incest because they left the child with the father, or uncle or older brother. It seems to me an extraordinary notion that the woman would be suspicious of these men, her relatives and friends. Can you imagine even thinking that such a thing could happen? The results of this mother-blaming is that the mother is often ostracised when the incest is discovered. I spoke to one woman whose daughter was molested by her husband, the child's stepfather, when the girl was in her early teens. 'Everyone felt I should have known. They blamed me for not knowing. Even my daughter felt that. They all treated me like dirt – the neighbours, our friends. Most people didn't believe it; everyone thought he was such a good bloke and when he denied it and went around telling everyone that my daughter and I were making it up, many believed him. Even when people found out it was true, they still blamed my daughter. It must have been her fault – she's that sort of girl, they said. And it started when she was only twelve.'

'When my daugher told me I just felt empty. Suddenly a lot of things fell into place and I knew she was telling the truth. I blame myself for the way I'd treated her – we hadn't been getting on at the time. I thought she was rebelling, you know what teenagers are like. That's why she hadn't told me and didn't tell me until it had been going on for years. But when it started I just had no idea.'

One wonders if the fact that mothers know they too will be blamed if the sexual abuse is made public is one reason they may fail to take action when told what's happening by the child. It's a natural self-protective mechanism to avoid putting yourself in a situation where you will be judged guilty – far easier to decide your child is making it up than face the consequence of what they are telling you.

Of course, for the family, the consequences of facing up to the incest are often horrendous. I remember receiving a letter from a woman whose husband was gaoled for incest. She argued passionately that despite the crime he had committed, the effects of his imprisonment on the family were far worse than any emotional damage which could have resulted from the incest. The children were teased and then rejected by school mates, the family ended up seeking refuge in a women's shelter, unable to support themselves. The emotional turmoil on all of them, guilt, blame, anger, revulsion, was amplified by the vicious gossiping and unwelcome public attention the family received.

The effects on the victim of reporting the crime can be especially devastating – often the girl will be removed from the family until the case is brought to trial. She ends up a double victim, treated with curiosity and suspicion by all who know her circumstances, with details of her private sexual life made public, destroying any chance of normal sexual development. It's no wonder that many families choose to cover up their family skeleton. One wonders what it must be like to be a woman who chooses to live with a man she knows has abused her own daughter. Perhaps often they have no choice, no escape. Are such women still able to forgive, to make love to such a man? As usual, we know little about the tangle of emotions which must exist in a family which lives with such a secret. There is so much we will never know or understand.

There are so many myths about child sexual abuse that it makes it hard for us to see and hear. There's the idea that it only happens to certain people; the poor, the uneducated, the underprivileged, *them*, rather than *us*. If we're married to lawyers and doctors, we imagine the child abuser as the unemployed layabout living on the other side of town. But the evidence is it happens everywhere, to every social group. Welfare workers tend to stumble across the problem more often in families where they have more work to do. When they are visiting homes to help with problems of unemployment or poverty or social problems, they are more likely to notice the withdrawn child who seems afraid of contact with adult males or the sexually provocative five-year-old. But when dad is well educated and well established, it's often just easier for him to hide what's going on. He has his study, he has his privacy – it's that much easier to keep it all hidden. And that much easier when the problem emerges for him to use his skills, his intelligence and his money to protect himself with lawyers, to pay to keep things quiet.

Janice's father was a psychologist in a small country town. He started molesting her when she was only three or four. He'd come into her bedroom, stand there with an erection and fondle her, rub his penis against her. From the beginning she knew that there was something wrong but daddy told her not to tell. 'It's just our little secret,' he'd say, 'don't tell mummy, she'll be cross with you, she'll be so hurt.' Janice tried to tell her mother. 'Oh don't be so stupid, Janice,' was the reply. So from then until she was about eight, it went on. He tried again when she was an adolescent but by then she could push him away. Yet she was still afraid to make a fuss, afraid of what would happen if she made the issue public. Here was this man, the psychologist everyone turned to for help, powerful, competent, admired, who would believe her? And there was always his little family joke, 'Oh you are quite mad, I'll have you put you away in a mental home.'

Talking to this woman, now in her thirties and still struggling to overcome her feelings of anger and resentment against males, it's obvious how devastating this experience was on her life and her relationships. She finds it very hard to maintain a relationship with a male and worries a great deal about how her past affects her ability to raise her four-year-old son. She is very nervous whenever a male in her life is close to her son and reacts by pushing him away – from both of them. Her trust is gone.

I have talked to many women like her who have had to work so hard to overcome years of self-blaming, and guilt, fear, powerlessness. It's easy to see why many women maintain their rage and never learn to feel secure in relationships with men. If your first close relationship, first sexual relationship is with an adult male who forces you to participate in sexual activity you don't understand and often don't enjoy, who makes you feel guilty and uses your guilt to manipulate you into keeping quiet, what hope is there for you ever to gain the confidence to have an equal loving relationship with a man? It is hardly surprising that sex therapists find their rooms filled with patients who have never been able to overcome the damaging effects of this introduction to their sexual lives. Dr Derek Richardson, former President of the Australian Society of Sex Educators, Researchers and Therapists, recently conducted a random survey of 150 patients attending his practice with sexual problems. Forty-three per cent of the female patients and 35 per cent of the male patients he surveyed had experienced sexual assault by a relative as a child. You would expect many of these people would experience sexual problems – but that's only the tip of the iceberg compared to the possible effects of their confidence, their relationships and perhaps their ability to be good parents to their own children.

It's easy to understand and feel angry. What is harder is to take that next step and force yourself to think about your own children and the men around you. It is so hard to accept that the men you know and love, those nice, ordinary, decent men can be misled by the secrecy that surrounds child abuse, and the myth that it really does no harm, into going that little bit too far. The only way we have of protecting children is to talk to each other about our own experiences, to break down the myths and convince people it happens, and to be vigilant. We'll start to protect children when we learn to believe them.

In the past few years, educational programmes have been established to teach children to protect themselves. The programmes are based on the assumption it is not always possible for adults to watch their children, but children must feel free to come and tell them if anyone tries to do anything to them they don't like.

One important part of these programmes is to teach children to trust their feelings, and when they feel something is wrong, to know they can tell another adult without fearing being blamed or punished. The programmes often start with pre-school children; they have found even two and three-year-olds can learn to protect themselves, to say 'no' and to tell other adults about sexual approach. These are some of the messages conveyed in the programme messages which every parent can start to teach their children.

Children need to be taught words to use to describe all parts of their bodies, particularly their genitals. By teaching them words to use, we are telling them it's okay to talk about their 'private' parts, and tell us if someone tries to touch them. Words can give permission to talk.

Children need to know they have a right to say 'no' if someone tries to touch them or is touching them in a way they don't like. In giving them this right, we must accept it if they don't want to kiss Aunty Harriet goodbye or don't want to sit on a stranger's knee or don't like being tickled. We must demonstrate this by backing them up if they don't want to do these things. They won't feel free to come to us if they have learnt we adults force them to kiss and touch people whether they like it or not. They have to learn to trust their feelings.

Children need to learn they don't *have* to keep secrets. You can talk about the difference between secrets and surprises-surprises are for birthdays and Christmas, for keeping quiet about presents. 'It's fun to have secrets with kids your own age. But secrets are something it's not fair for an older child or adult to make you keep. Sometimes secrets are hiding things that shouldn't be hidden.'

If someone does touch a child or does something to them which confuses them, they need to know it's not their fault and even if it's already happened they can still come and tell. They must know they can always come and check even if they felt at the time that everything was okay.

Children can be taught 'what if' games which include situations where they are at risk. Ask your child, 'If you were walking down the street and someone asked you to come inside their house to see the new kittens, what would you do?' Most children would answer 'Go and see the kittens.' You can use this sort of game to guide children to the answer you would like. 'I would say, "no, thank you, I have to ask my mum first".' You can ask other question such as, 'What if a babysitter asked you to undress so you could play a special secret game with him?' If these questions are mixed up with other 'what if' questions, they won't seem frightening or unusual, for example 'What if you wanted to telephone from a call box and didn't have any money?'

Gay Children

It has happened more than once. I've picked up the telephone to be greeted by the sound of a woman sobbing, a cry for help from someone who had no one else to talk to. The problem? She had discovered her son (or daughter) is a homosexual. The mothers call me, overwhelmed with guilt and remorse, trying to find out what they may have done, where did they go wrong?

It is always very sad for me as a psychologist to talk to such parents and realise how much my own profession has contributed to their distress and feelings of guilt and shame. For many years psychiatrists and psychologists believed family background was an important cause of what they saw as the 'sickness' of homosexuality. They hunted for theories to identify types of childrearing which could cause a change in sexual orientation and always it was the parents who were to blame. Some psychologists thought the mother was too dominating, the father too affectionate and weak. Others believed the problem was a father who was absent or unavailable. Sometimes the theory was that the mother was too controlling or too close to her son, too distant from her daughter. There were dozens of theories, all contradicting each other and all leaving parents racked with guilt about the damage they had caused. The irony is that after inducing all this guilt the professionals have changed their minds. First they decided that homosexuality was not an illness. In the early 1970s the world's professional psychiatric associations removed homosexuality from the list of mental disorders. As someone commented, 'never in history had so many people been cured in so little time'. Since then there has been steadily accumulating evidence suggesting that parental upbringing has nothing to do with causing homosexuality. We just don't know why some people are attracted to their own sex but it seems homosexuals are born rather than made.

The trouble is that not everyone has caught up with the psychiatric profession's turnabout, and there are many people in our community who still believe homosexuality is an illness caused by parental upbringing. This means that not only do parents of homosexuals start off by blaming themselves but even if they do finally accept they aren't the cause of their children's sexual orientation, they live in a society which still holds them responsible. Myths take a long time to die.

As editor of the gay publication, *OutRage*, Danny Vadasz has spent many years counselling parents to cope with the discovery of homosexual children. He believes that, while many homosexuals have now found support through the various gay organisations, it is their parents who are left floundering; 'The coming out, the liberation that has occurred for gays in the past ten or fifteen years has lifted the pressure that has been on their shoulders, making them feel less isolated and part of a strong gay community. But that pressure hasn't disappeared. In many cases it has simply shifted on to the shoulders of their parents who have to cope without any of the support now offered to their offspring. The more visible gays become, the more their parents are exposed to the public glare.'

Since most of the parents have been brought up to think of homosexuality as a form of 'mental disorder', which is condemned by society, they naturally agonise over the welfare of a son or daughter who may be forced to live as an outcast. We all see television shows such as 'Are You Being Served?' and 'The Benny

Hill Show' where homosexuals are the object of ridicule and derision. How hard it must be to suddenly imagine your son or daughter being treated like that. Unfortunately, there are many myths about homosexuality which contribute to the fear parents feel for their children. There are many false stereotypes: the effeminate man (who wants to be a woman); the muscular woman (who wants to be a man); the ineffectual, sick weaklings who couldn't hold down a job, or shouldn't be allowed to. The result is many parents fear their children will never have a good home, a normal family life, that they will never know love, they will automatically be excluded from successful careers, or that they will be outcasts and misfits, harrassed and looked down on all their lives, ending up lonely and unhappy.

Now there is an even greater fear, particularly for parents of gay sons, the fear of a life-threatening disease – AIDS. There are now groups in many states like the Melbourne-based Parents and Friends of Gays Association, which help parents deal with such issues. These groups are designed to help dispel some of the myths about the homosexual lifestyle, and to provide realistic and accurate information about issues such as AIDS. The groups also include gay people of all ages so that parents can talk to homosexuals about what their lives are like, can meet happy, confident, successful homosexual men and women and realise that it is possible for their children to have productive, happy lives.

There are also homosexual organisations all over Australia operating telephone counselling services where gay counsellors answer many of the questions parents have about the effects of a homosexual lifestyle. A telephone call, reading books, talking to parents in similar situations – it can be the beginning of a painful process of acceptance for the parent who wants help and who also wants to help.

Unfortunately, there are also many parents who find the truth just too difficult to accept. Many young men and women tell distressing stories of parents who just didn't want to hear. One lesbian visited her mother one morning especially to tell her about being gay. 'My goodness, cabbages are expensive at the market today, dear,' said mum busily packing away the groceries. 'Mum, there's something I have to tell you. I'm a lesbian.' 'Eighty-five cents,' came the reply. 'It's a disgrace.'

More often it is the father who has difficulty accepting what is happening and who just doesn't want to know. Many homosexuals, male and female, tell their mothers first. As Danny Vadasz points out, most mothers have a wonderful ability to accept anything in their children – 'just as long as they are happy'. And once they finally accept that, through no fault of their own, their child is homosexual, they usually learn to cope.

For a father, the discovery that he has a homosexual son is a threat to his masculinity. First there's the guilt about being a proper parent. 'I should have played football more with him or taken him fishing.' Guilt about being the absent father; 'I should have come home earlier from work.' Sometimes they blame their wives, 'You coddled the boy . . . treated him like a baby. I told you not to teach him to cook.' But underneath all that there's also the threat to their own masculinity. 'If I produce a gay son, what does that say about *me*?'

Sometimes this threat causes the father to react aggressively as he struggles to acknowledge his feelings. Many gay sons and their mothers recognise the difficulty the father of the family will have coming to terms with the situation, and decide to keep the truth from the father. It places an extraordinary stress on a mother to have to keep such a secret from her husband but often she knows it is the only solution. Others try to tell fathers. It doesn't always work. One mother and her gay son set up a special dinner to break the news to dad. After a relaxing meal, mum left the room and the son said, 'Dad, there's something I want to tell you.' Father said, '*Look*, if you mean you want to talk about being a poofter, I know. But I don't want to talk about it.' When pressed to discuss the subject by his son, he reacted so violently the son never dared mention the subject again.

Parents often don't realise how much courage it has taken to make this confession. As Danny Vadasz points out, even if you know you have a good relationship with your parents you can never be sure how they will react; 'I was very nervous. It was the most frightening thing I had ever faced. The risk factor is enormous. Even though you have confidence in your relationship with your parents there's that almighty fear that they are going to reject you. I know I just couldn't cope if they had done that.'

Some children choose to protect their parents by keeping their homosexual relationships hidden and making a pretence of dating the opposite sex. Yet they may well be planting evidence to give the game away, leaving notes, phone numbers which could be easily detected – all in a desperate attempt to bring the whole thing out into the open. Other young people leave home, or even-run away, to avoid facing the inevitable confrontation with their parents. In any group of runaway kids haunting places like Sydney's King Cross, there are gay adolescents who left home to avoid their parents' discovering they were homosexual.

Unfortunately, when parents are kept ignorant, the chances are they will learn the truth in the worst possible circumstances. Your nosey next door neighbour sees your son and friend through the window of a gay bar. You walk unannounced into your daughter's flat and discover her flatmate shares her bed. Worse, there are now parents who discover their son is homosexual at the same time as learning he has contracted AIDS. For a parent, it is difficult enough at any time to provide support for a mortally-ill son. To do so while dealing with all the guilt, self-blame and confusion which surrounds the issue of homosexual children, is an extremely tall order. In some cases, the gravity of the situation helps parents come to terms with issues they would otherwise have found hard to accept – they are more willing to accept their son's friends and partners when forced to combine together to provide support and encouragement for the ill man. Others can't cope – and their rejection becomes just one more, often intolerable, burden for the AIDS sufferer.

Even parents who are willing and able to accept their children's homosexuality are still aware that others around them are less tolerant. It is often difficult for parents to know to whom to reveal the truth. One mother, after a great deal of agonising, finally told her ninety-year-old mother that her daughter didn't just have a flat mate, she had a female lover. 'That's nice dear,' was the calm reply. But often there are family members and friends who would find it just too difficult to cope with the situation if they were openly confronted with the truth. Even younger people, siblings, have their individual reactions. Many siblings are very supportive. Teachers even tell stories of nine and ten-year-olds talking proudly of their gay brothers in 'show-and-tell' sessions at schools. Others, caught in that self-conscious adolescent stage, reject their homosexual sibling because they are afraid it will affect their own social standing.

In larger families there is always the chance that more than one child will be homosexual. Estimates of the incidence of homosexuality vary but research suggests up to 10 per cent of the population have considerable homosexual experience. This means homosexuality will touch a large proportion of families. On the basis of these figures you would expect 10 per cent of one child families, more than one-sixth of families with two children, one-quarter of families with three children and about one-third of families with four children to have one or more homosexual children. You would also predict 2 per cent of three child families and 3 per cent of four child families to have two or more homosexual children.

Two gay siblings – it's purely a coincidence but as you would imagine, it's one which parents find particularly hard to accept. Danny Vadasz once spent months counselling a woman who had just discovered her son was gay. After numerous telephone calls she finally stopped blaming herself and accepted his homosexuality. He didn't hear from her for a few months then suddenly came another call. There she was again, sobbing into the phone, 'You know I rang you before and talked about Barry, well Ed's gay too . . . so it *must* have been me.' One son she could accept as a coincidence, but *two sons* – it must have been something she had done wrong.

Even with one child, after the initial discovery there are still many issues which need to be confronted. For many parents the fact that your child is unlikely to produce grandchildren is the cause of great sadness. (There *are* many lesbian parents – homosexual men and women who marry and rear children before discovering or coming to terms with their homosexuality or more recently, lesbian mothers who conceive through artificial insemination. In other countries it is also possible for homosexual couples to adopt children.) It is often difficult for families to accept the son or daughter's homosexual partner and invite the couple to family gatherings – yet it is precisely this sort of acceptance that the homosexual person is often desperately seeking from his family. It is most distressing for a gay man or woman to find their loved partner excluded from family events – where even the worst of the family's black sheep are made welcome.

There is so much for a parent to learn and try to accept. Even the idea of two men or two women loving each other is alien when you have been brought up in a heterosexual society. As one mother of a gay son commented, 'You just don't understand it. Even the physical act of two men making love you just don't understand because you've never been exposed to it and that's something that can really stun you. I mean, to try to visualise your son in situations of intimacy is hard, because you don't see men kissing.'

For many parents, it's tempting to cling to the hope that their offspring's homosexuality is only a passing phase. Many adolescents are attracted to their own sex – it can be purely a stage in their sexual development – but homosexuals usually are aware from this early age that their sexual preferences are directly towards their own sex, and they stay this way. There's no point in trying to force a homosexual to behave as a heterosexual – many marriages have floundered when a homosexual partner can no longer cope with the deceit of being married to someone for whom he or she feels no physical attraction. There's also no point in forcing your son or daughter to talk to a doctor or seek psychiatric help. These days it is extremely unlikely that you would find a professional person willing to attempt to change a person's sexual orientation. Previous attempts – using psychotherapy, behaviour and aversion therapy, have generally proved totally unsuccessful, simply increasing the guilt and anxiety which prevents homosexuals from living happy, productive lives.

In the end, the best thing a parent can do is to talk to other parents in similar circumstances, to learn about the homosexual lifestyle, to try to accept your child and offer your support. Parental acceptance is immensely important in helping many homosexuals cope with the difficulties inherent in their lifestyle. As one young homosexual woman commented to me; 'It was awful watching my parents trying to cope with their feelings when they discovered I was gay. But they finally learnt to accept me for what I am and now their love and support is one of my most important assets. We are closer now than we ever were before. So many barriers have come down.'

Also published by Penguin

Health and Australian Society
Basil S. Hetzel

Most Australians regard themselves as healthy. Basil Hetzel, however, shows that the popular image of the healthy, tanned athlete is a myth. Indeed, by generally accepted health standards, Australians are among the least healthy groups living in 'developed' societies.

Health and Australian Society aims to increase everyone's understanding of health and urgent health problems. It presents and analyses the basic information on the health status of Australians and the major health problems of coronary heart disease, cancer, excess alcohol consumption, cigarette smoking and the 'affluent' diet. In this revised edition, the new developments in health promotion, the finance of health care, the planning of medical manpower and services are examined.

Life style changes are necessary – and possible – to improve health, and life expectancy can be increased as people learn to take responsibility for their health.

Not the Marrying Kind
Robyn Penman and Yvonne Stolk

How and why do women live without being wives to men and mothers to children? How atypical are these women who opt to remain single?

Not the Marrying Kind explores the contradictions between the traditional view of 'spinsters' and the evidence gathered in a survey of unmarried, childless Australian women. As the myth has it, these women should be unfulfilled, desperate, impaired people – but they're not. The problem is that such beliefs persist without basis because they are in accord with a set of false assumptions about the nature and status of women, thus restricting women and men in their life options.

In refuting the mythology, the authors open the way for a new consideration of the alternatives and the real choices available to everyone.

Tall Poppies
Susan Mitchell

How does a woman become successful in Australia today?

Susan Mitchell asked nine such women that question. They talk candidly and intimately about their professional and private lives, about what it's like to enjoy success and what it took to achieve it. They reveal the secrets behind their public lives and the many painful and difficult choices they had to make along the way.

A refugee who, with marriage and motherhood, became Businesswoman of the Year; a gawky schoolgirl, now a popular television personality, model and fashion designer; an Aboriginal who fought racism to become head of a government department – these and the six other equally remarkable women who make up this book stand tall for us all.

Joy Baluch, Beatrice Faust, Pat Lovell, Eve Mahlab, Robyn Nevin, Pat O'Shane, Elizabeth Riddell, Mima Stojanovic, Maggie Tabberer

Even in the Best of Homes
Jocelynne Scutt

The family has long been seen as a haven of help, comfort, affection and goodwill, shielded from a heartless world. But too often, it is a facade concealing violence and abuse meted out by husbands to wives, and fathers (and sometimes mothers) to children.

Jocelynne Scutt's study of Australian families revealed the beating, rape and murder of wives, the bashing and sexual molestation of children – and the apathy of friends, family, doctors, police and the courts. In any other situation, these acts of violence would be regarded as serious crimes, but because they occur within the family, usually in the privacy of the home, people are reluctant to 'interfere'.

The abuse will stop only when the laws to protect people are properly enforced, when women gain public and private autonomy, and when children are regarded as human beings, not property.

Mothers and Working Mothers
Jan Harper and Lyn Richards

It was me or them. I was going to become submerged by children. (Working mother)

It's always been the husband who goes out to work . . . women are more suited to looking after children than men. (Mother at home)

Neither the mother at home nor the 'working mother' feels that society clearly approves her choice. If she stays home she's 'lazy' but if she goes to work she's 'selfish'.

In this book, two sociologists who are themselves mothers tackle an issue of lively concern to Australian families: how and when a mother decides whether or not to work outside the home.

From the mid-1960s to the mid-1970s there was a dramatic increase in the participation of married women in the paid workforce. But during the next decade this friend stopped. In the introduction to the 1985 edition Lyn Richards examines and discusses the latest statistics.

Like its companion volume, *Having Families* (revised edition, 1985) by Lyn Richards, *Mothers and Working Mothers* is based on research funded by the Royal Commission on Human Relationships.

The Heartache of Motherhood
Joyce Nicholson

Joyce Nicholson is the mother of four grown-up children. After thirty-five years of devoted marriage, she left the family home to live alone – happily.

This book is a deeply personal account of her feelings about being a mother; her honesty is extraordinary and very moving, her conclusions startling.

'The problem is that no one prepares you for the awful side of motherhood'; for the loneliness, the guilt, the constant worry, the financial dependence on a man, the loss of self-confidence, the boredom. Of course there are good things too – the sweetness of babyhood, friendship with growing children, the pleasure of shared experiences. But the fact remains that for many women motherhood provides more heartache than joy.

'An important and passionate book' *Fay Weldon*